MASTERING THE SERIES 6 & 63 EXAM

MASTERING THE SERIES 6 & 63 EXAM

Written By

D.W. LINDSEY

Mastering the Series 6 & 63 Exam
D.W. Lindsey

First Edition, 2025

TABLE OF CONTENTS

PREFACE
INTRODUCTION TO SECURITIES LICENSING

If you're holding this book, chances are you're standing at the edge of a new opportunity—a career in the financial services industry. Whether you're hoping to become a registered representative, a financial advisor, or part of a broader investment team, passing the Series 6 and 63 exams is your gateway.

In the United States, anyone who wants to sell mutual funds, variable annuities, or other packaged investment products must be licensed. These licenses are not just bureaucratic checkboxes—they're designed to ensure that professionals in the securities industry understand how to serve their clients responsibly, ethically, and legally.

The Series 6 license, administered by FINRA (Financial Industry Regulatory Authority), qualifies individuals to solicit, purchase, and/or sell specific types of investment products. The Series 63 license, governed by NASAA (North American Securities Administrators Association), focuses on state law and is required by most states to legally conduct business with clients. Together, they open the door to a world of professional opportunities.

IMPORTANCE OF SERIES 6 & 63 CERTIFICATIONS

These certifications are often the first step toward a rewarding and meaningful career in finance. They prove not only your technical knowledge of securities products and laws but also your commitment to ethical practice and fiduciary duty.

Employers look for candidates who are **licensed**—or are actively pursuing their licenses—because it shows initiative. Clients feel more secure knowing you've passed industry-standard tests. And perhaps most importantly, you gain confidence in your ability to advise, educate, and protect the people who trust you with their financial future.

Passing both exams isn't just about memorizing facts. It's about building a professional foundation that will serve you for years to come. This book is designed to help you do just that—efficiently, confidently, and on the first try.

HOW TO USE THIS BOOK EFFECTIVELY

This isn't just a textbook. It's a study coach, a resource bank, and a guide through the maze of licensing preparation.

The book is divided into four major parts:

Part I gives you a strong overview of both exams, their structure, and smart study strategies.

Part II focuses on the Series 6 exam: product knowledge, client interaction, regulations, and transaction processing.

Part III dives into the Series 63 exam: state laws, ethical practices, and advisor responsibilities.

Part IV includes practice questions, mock exams, and detailed answer explanations—so you can test your knowledge and identify any weak spots before test day.

At the end of the book, you'll also find appendices with a glossary of terms, quick-reference concepts, and final tips to maximize your performance.

Here's our deal: You commit to a focused, consistent study plan—and this book will guide you through every step. Each chapter is designed with clarity in mind, and you'll find plenty of reminders, examples, and real-world applications along the way. Whether you're a brand-new graduate or making a mid-career change, this book is for you. Let's get you licensed—and launched.

CHAPTER 1

OVERVIEW OF SERIES 6 AND SERIES 63

INTRODUCTION: OPENING THE DOOR TO A FINANCIAL CAREER

If you're preparing for the Series 6 and 63 exams, you're not just studying for a test—you're investing in a professional future.

These two certifications are often the first step into the world of financial advising and securities sales. Whether you're entering the workforce for the first time, making a career shift, or expanding your current role, passing the Series 6 and 63 exams is a foundational milestone. But before diving into charts, products, and laws, it's critical to understand why these exams exist, how they differ, and what you need to do to qualify for them.

This chapter will walk you through the purpose, scope, differences, and registration process for both exams—so you can begin your prep with clarity and confidence.

THE PURPOSE AND SCOPE OF EACH EXAM

The Series 6 and Series 63 exams are essential entry points into the U.S. financial services industry, particularly for professionals looking to sell mutual funds, variable annuities, and other packaged investment products. Each exam serves a distinct regulatory purpose and is governed by different regulatory bodies.

The Series 6 – Investment Company and Variable Contracts Products Representative Exam

The Series 6, administered by the Financial Industry Regulatory Authority (FINRA), qualifies individuals to function as a limited representative. This designation permits them to solicit, purchase, and sell specific securities products including:

✓ Mutual funds
✓ Unit investment trusts (UITs)
✓ Variable annuities
✓ Variable life insurance products
✓ Municipal fund securities (e.g., 529 plans)

It does not allow professionals to sell individual stocks, options, or corporate debt securities — those fall under Series 7 licensing.

The Series 6 is ideal for those planning to become investment company product representatives, insurance agents, or financial advisors working in environments that emphasize packaged products.

THE SERIES 63 – UNIFORM SECURITIES AGENT STATE LAW EXAMINATION

The Series 63 is developed by the North American Securities Administrators Association (NASAA) and administered by FINRA. Its purpose is state law compliance. While the Series 6 focuses on what you sell, the Series 63 governs how and where you're legally permitted to do so within each U.S. state.

Passing the Series 63:

✓ Satisfies state-level registration requirements for securities agents

✓ Emphasizes ethical conduct, fiduciary responsibilities, and state regulations

✓ Is required by most states in addition to Series 6, 7, or other FINRA exams

In short, while the Series 6 lets you sell certain financial products, the Series 63 ensures you can do so lawfully and ethically within each state.

KEY DIFFERENCES AND SIMILARITIES

Though both exams are often taken together, they differ in scope, content, regulatory jurisdiction, and purpose. Understanding these distinctions will help you approach your preparation with clarity.

Feature	Series 6	Series 63
Administered by	FINRA	FINRA (on behalf of NASAA)
Primary Focus	Investment company products & variable contracts	State securities laws & ethical standards
Product Coverage	Mutual funds, UITs, variable annuities/life	Not product-specific
Licensing Result	Limited Representative	State-Level Registration (Agent)
Role Type	Salesperson/advisor	Legal and compliance adherence
Pre-requisites	Sponsorship by FINRA-member firm	Often required along with Series 6 or 7

Similarities:

✓ Both require sponsorship (for Series 6) or firm affiliation (for Series 63, post-license)

✓ Both are computer-based multiple-choice exams

✓ Both demand strong understanding of rules, ethics, and financial instruments

ELIGIBILITY AND REGISTRATION PROCESS

Understanding how to qualify for each exam and how to register can save you from unnecessary delays. Here's what you need to know.

Eligibility Requirements for the Series 6

Sponsorship Required: You must be sponsored by a FINRA-member firm to register for the Series 6. This typically means securing a job offer or being hired into a training program.

Form U4: Your employer files a Uniform Application for Securities Industry Registration or Transfer (Form U4) on your behalf via FINRA's Central Registration Depository (CRD) system.

Background Check: Filing Form U4 initiates a criminal background and financial history check.

Exam Fee: As of this writing, the Series 6 exam fee is $75, though this may change.

Eligibility for the Series 63
No Sponsorship Required: Unlike the Series 6, you may take the Series 63 without firm sponsorship, though most candidates take it while affiliated with a firm.

Registration Process: Individuals register directly or through their employer via the FINRA website.

The Series 63 exam fee is around $147.
State Approval: Passing the exam does not guarantee you can immediately conduct business in all states—you must apply for state-specific registration through your firm.

WHY YOU NEED BOTH LICENSES

You'll often hear that the **Series 6 and 63** "go hand in hand"—and for good reason. Most financial professionals working in retail securities need both to operate fully.

For example:
If you're advising a client in New York on mutual fund purchases, you need the Series 6 to sell the product and the Series 63 to meet New York state licensing requirements.

Even if you don't actively advise clients, if you accept orders or process paperwork, you may still be subject to both licensing requirements.

The combination of Series 6 and 63 ensures that:
✓ You understand both product rules (Series 6) and state legal standards (Series 63)
✓ You are qualified and authorized in most states to act as a securities agent
✓ You reduce regulatory and compliance risk to your firm

WHO TAKES THESE EXAMS—AND WHY?

These exams are taken by:
✓ Aspiring financial advisors
✓ Insurance agents expanding into securities
✓ Customer service representatives transitioning into sales roles
✓ New hires at brokerage firms or independent advisory firms
✓ Career changers from banking, accounting, or teaching

If your career goal involves:
✓ Helping individuals with long-term investment planning
✓ Selling packaged products
✓ Working with retirement accounts or college savings plans

...then these licenses are likely non-negotiable.

TEST-DAY EXPERIENCE: WHAT TO EXPECT

Here's a quick preview of what you can expect on exam day:

- ✓ Exams are delivered at Prometric test centers or online through remote proctoring
- ✓ Each test includes:
- ✓ A tutorial period
- ✓ A defined time limit (90 minutes for Series 6; 75 minutes for Series 63)
- ✓ Multiple-choice questions only
- ✓ You'll receive an immediate pass/fail score report at the end of the exam
- ✓ Passing both on your first try is achievable with a focused plan, and this book is designed to help you get there.

COMMON MYTHS AND MISUNDERSTANDINGS

"Series 6 is just a basic test—you don't need to study that hard."
False. The Series 6 may seem "easier" than the Series 7, but many candidates fail for underestimating the content, especially around ethics, regulations, and product suitability.

"Series 63 isn't important—I'll focus only on Series 6."
Dangerous mindset. Many states require Series 63 before you can legally engage with clients, even if you're technically licensed under Series 6.

"Once I pass, I'm set for life."
Not quite. You'll need to maintain your license through continuing education, and your firm must keep you registered and in good standing.

FINAL THOUGHTS: STARTING YOUR JOURNEY RIGHT

By now, you should understand:

- ✓ The distinct role each exam plays
- ✓ Why both are necessary for most financial roles
- ✓ What it takes to become eligible and registered
- ✓ The types of professionals who benefit from passing them
- ✓ Your preparation journey will demand discipline, strategic planning, and the right resources. The next chapter will dive into the structure and format of each exam so you know exactly how to prepare.
- ✓ You're not just studying — you're opening the door to a rewarding, respected profession.

CHAPTER 2
EXAM STRUCTURES AND FORMATS

Most exam takers underestimate the value of understanding the **structure** and **format** of an exam. But the Series 6 and Series 63 are not tests of raw intelligence or memorization alone—they are tests of strategy. You may master all the investment concepts and legal regulations, but if you mismanage your time, second-guess formats, or misread the scoring system, your performance could suffer.

In this chapter, we will break down:

- The format, timing, and structure of the Series 6 and Series 63
- How questions are designed and what that means for your strategy
- Scoring methodology, including what counts, what doesn't, and what's required to pass
- Exam-day experience, including the psychological factors and administrative logistics that can impact success
- This knowledge is more than technical—it's tactical. Once you understand the framework, you can train like a professional, simulate real conditions, and walk into the exam with confidence.

SECTION 1: SERIES 6 EXAM BREAKDOWN

Exam Format and Structure

Feature	Details
Number of Questions	50 Multiple-Choice Questions
Exam Duration	90 Minutes (1 hour, 30 minutes)
Format	Computer-Based
Type of Questions	4-option Multiple Choice
Scoring	Must score at least 70% to pass
Delivery Method	Prometric Test Center or Online

CONTENT BREAKDOWN BY FUNCTION

The Series 6 exam isn't organized randomly—it follows a job task analysis. FINRA categorizes the 50 questions across four key functions of a registered representative's role:

Function	Description	# of Questions
Function 1	Seeks business for the broker-dealer through customers and potential customers	12
Function 2	Opens accounts after obtaining and evaluating customers' financial profile and investment objectives	8
Function 3	Provides customers with information about investments, makes suitable recommendations, transfers assets, and maintains appropriate records	15
Function 4	Obtains and verifies customers' purchase and sale instructions; processes, completes and confirms transactions	15

Understanding this breakdown is essential. You can't afford to over-prepare for Function 2 and neglect Function 3, which has more weight. Your study plan should align proportionally with this distribution.

TYPES OF QUESTIONS AND WHAT THEY TEST

1. Scenario-Based Questions
You'll often be presented with a short case study:
"A 58-year-old client nearing retirement seeks stable income and low risk. Which product is most suitable?"

These questions test your ability to apply suitability standards—a major theme in Series 6.

2. Terminology & Concept Questions
"What is the surrender charge on a variable annuity?"

Expect straightforward definition and recall items that test technical understanding.

3. Regulatory and Rule-Based Questions
"Which disclosure is required when recommending mutual fund Class B shares?"

These questions test your grasp of FINRA, SEC, and internal compliance rules.

TEST INTERFACE & TOOLS

The Series 6 test interface includes:
✓ A flag option for marking questions to revisit
✓ An on-screen calculator
✓ A built-in tutorial (which does not count against your time)

You are allowed to skip questions and return, which allows you to prioritize time. A best practice is to answer easier questions first, mark harder ones, and circle back.

SCORING AND PERFORMANCE METRICS

Passing Score: 70% (i.e., 35 out of 50 scored questions must be correct)

Pretest Questions: Included within the 50, but undisclosed. These are *trial questions* being tested for future exams and do not count toward your score—but you won't know which ones they are.

Important: You could technically answer 38 questions correctly, but if three of those were unscored pretest questions, your official score would be 35—exactly passing.

This is why you must treat every question as if it counts.

SECTION 2: SERIES 63 EXAM BREAKDOWN

Overview of the Series 63 Exam

The Series 63, or *Uniform Securities Agent State Law Examination*, is governed by NASAA and also administered by FINRA. It focuses on:

✓ State securities regulations
✓ Anti-fraud provisions
✓ Ethical practices
✓ Agent-client interactions

It's required by most U.S. states to legally offer or solicit the sale of securities.

EXAM FORMAT AND STRUCTURE

Feature	Details
Number of Questions	65 Total Questions (60 Scored + 5 Unscored)
Exam Duration	75 Minutes (1 hour, 15 minutes)

Format	Computer-Based
Question Type	4-option Multiple Choice
Passing Score	72% (i.e., 43 out of 60 scored questions)
Delivery Method	Prometric Test Center or Online

CONTENT BREAKDOWN

The Series 63 doesn't follow the job-task format like the Series 6. Instead, NASAA structures the content around core legal and regulatory concepts, including:

✓ Registration of persons and securities
✓ Business practices and fiduciary obligations
✓ Unethical and dishonest conduct
✓ Remedies and penalties for violations

Unlike Series 6, these topics are not disclosed with specific question counts, which makes holistic study essential.

COMMON QUESTION FORMATS

1. Rule-Based Scenarios

"Under the Uniform Securities Act, which of the following transactions would be exempt?"

These questions evaluate your legal understanding of exemptions, registration, and compliance.

2. Ethical Dilemmas

"An agent finds out a client is terminally ill. Is it ethical to recommend a variable life policy?"

Tests your ethical decision-making and understanding of fiduciary duty.

3. Trick Questions or Reversals

Expect reverse logic:

"All of the following are prohibited practices EXCEPT…"

Be careful with wording. Always underline or note key qualifiers.

SCORING DETAILS AND PRETEST QUESTIONS

✓ 60 Questions are Scored
✓ 5 Questions are Pretest Questions – not counted in final score
✓ Passing Score = 72% → You must get 43 out of 60 correct

Again, since you don't know which 5 are unscored, every question must be treated seriously.

SECTION 3: TEST-DAY STRATEGIES AND PSYCHOLOGICAL PREPARATION

Know Your Pace

To finish comfortably:
✓ Series 6: ~1.8 minutes per question
✓ Series 63: ~1.15 minutes per question

Some questions will take longer; others less. Practice timed mock exams to develop internal pacing.

WHAT TO EXPECT AT THE TESTING CENTER

✓ Bring two forms of ID
✓ No personal items allowed; lockers are provided
✓ You'll be monitored by a camera and/or live proctor
✓ You'll sign an attestation form acknowledging the FINRA/NASAA test integrity policies

REMOTE EXAM OPTION

✓ FINRA now allows remote testing for most locations. Requirements:
✓ Private, quiet testing room
✓ High-speed internet
✓ Webcam, microphone, and compatible OS
✓ Room sweep at start of test
✓ The remote option is convenient but comes with higher technical risk, so ensure your setup is reliable.

FINAL WORDS: READINESS IS MASTERY

Understanding the test structure is a huge mental advantage. You now know:

✓ What to expect
✓ How long you have
✓ How the questions are arranged
✓ How scoring works

In the next Chapter, we'll build on this by teaching you how to study effectively, plan your schedule, and use the best prep materials in the industry.

CHAPTER 3
STUDY STRATEGIES AND RESOURCES

Passing the Series 6 and Series 63 exams ***doesn't come down to luck***—it comes down to **discipline, planning, and using the right tools**. These exams are structured to challenge not only your knowledge but your ability to apply concepts under time pressure. Whether you're balancing a full-time job, switching careers, or starting fresh, the path to success begins with a **smart, structured study strategy**.

This chapter is your comprehensive guide to:
✓ Crafting a study plan tailored to your life
✓ Choosing the right study materials
✓ Applying proven time-management techniques

The goal is not just to help you pass—but to ensure you walk into test day feeling fully prepared and confident.

SECTION 1: CREATING AN EFFECTIVE STUDY PLAN

1.1 Start with a Diagnostic

Before you start "studying," you need to **assess your current knowledge base**.

Why Take a Diagnostic Exam?
✓ Identifies strengths and weaknesses
✓ Guides topic prioritization
✓ Mimics real test conditions
✓ Serves as a baseline to measure progress

Use a free online Series 6 or 63 practice test or a sample from a prep provider. Time yourself and simulate exam conditions as closely as possible.

1.2 Define Your Timeframe

Your study plan depends on how much time you have before the test:

6–8 Weeks: Ideal timeframe for most candidates
4 Weeks or Less: Requires accelerated schedule and high commitment
3+ Months: Allows more flexibility and deeper understanding

1.3 Set Realistic Weekly Goals

Break your time into **weekly study blocks**. For example:

Week	Focus	Goal
Week 1	Overview + Diagnostic	Understand format, set goals
Week 2–4	Core Content (Series 6 & 63)	Read materials, take topic quizzes
Week 5	Practice exams & review weaknesses	Reinforce problem areas
Week 6	Final review + test simulations	Master timing and test strategy

Adjust the length depending on your schedule and test date.

1.4 Use the 80/20 Study Rule

The **Pareto Principle (80/20 Rule)** applies beautifully here:

80% of your results come from 20% of your focus areas.

✓ Prioritize high-weighted content areas (e.g., suitability questions in Series 6)
✓ Focus on repeat concepts (e.g., registration requirements in Series 63)
✓ Don't get bogged down in obscure facts with low exam relevance

1.5 Mix Passive and Active Learning

Passive reading alone won't cut it. Combine multiple learning styles:

Method	Benefit
Reading	Builds foundational understanding
Flashcards	Reinforces memory retention
Practice questions	Applies knowledge in exam format
Teaching others	Deepens understanding through explanation
Mnemonics	Simplifies complex info into mental triggers

1.6 Set Milestones and Rewards

Create **mini-**deadlines and reward checkpoints:

✓ Complete a chapter? Take a quiz.
✓ Score 80% on a mock test? Take a day off.
✓ Finish all your practice questions? Treat yourself.

These small wins maintain motivation and momentum.

SECTION 2: RECOMMENDED STUDY MATERIALS

The quality of your study resources can make or break your success. The Series 6 and 63 content may not be inherently difficult—but the way it's tested is nuanced and requires high-quality prep materials.

2.1 Official Exam Content Outlines

Always download the latest Series 6 and 63 Content Outlines directly from:

✓ FINRA.org (Series 6)
✓ NASAA.org (Series 63)

These outlines list the **exact topics** you'll be tested on and form the blueprint for all reputable prep guides.

2.2 Prep Books and Providers

The following are among the most trusted Series 6 & 63 prep sources:

Provider	Features
Kaplan Financial	Comprehensive textbooks, QBank, video courses
STC (Securities Training Corporation)	Great for structured programs with tutor support
Pass Perfect	Deep content dives, great analytics
ExamFX	More interactive and affordable, best for visual learners
Solomon Exam Prep	Shorter, targeted content ideal for re-takers or fast learners

Choose based on your learning style:
✓ Love to read? Go with Kaplan or Pass Perfect.
✓ Need video instruction? Try STC or ExamFX.
✓ Want gamified learning? Consider Solomon.

2.3 Flashcards & Apps

Repetition is key to retention. Digital or physical flashcards are ideal for mobile study moments. Try:

✓ Quizlet
✓ Brainscape
✓ Kaplan Flashcard App

Tip: Make your own flashcards while studying. The process of creating them cements knowledge.

2.4 Online Practice Exams

You must simulate the real exam several times before test day. Use practice tools with:

✓ Timer-enabled mock exams
✓ Performance analytics
✓ Detailed answer explanations

Take at least 3 full-length practice exams before test day and aim to score 80% or higher consistently.

2.5 Audio and Visual Resources

If you learn better through your ears or eyes:

✓ Watch YouTube videos explaining tricky concepts like variable annuity charges or Uniform Securities Act provisions
✓ Use podcasts that recap exam topics while driving or walking

Popular resources:
✓ Series 6 & 63 Exam Podcast (Spotify or Apple)
✓ Achievable YouTube Reviews
✓ Investopedia tutorials

SECTION 3: TIME MANAGEMENT TECHNIQUES

3.1 Make a Weekly Study Schedule

If you're working full-time or juggling life commitments, you'll need a schedule that respects your capacity.

Day	Task	Time Needed
Mon–Fri	Read 1–2 chapters, flashcards	1–1.5 hrs./day
Saturday	Practice test + review answers	3–4 hrs.
Sunday	Review missed questions, plan	2 hrs.

Consistency beats intensity. A daily habit, even if brief, trumps marathon cramming sessions.

3.2 Use the Pomodoro Technique

Study in **25-minute focused sprints** with 5-minute breaks.

✓ Helps prevent burnout
✓ Improves retention and energy

After four cycles, take a longer 15–30 minute break.

3.3 Block out Distractions

Digital distractions are silent killers of productivity. Use:

✓ Website blockers (e.g., Cold Turkey, Freedom)
✓ Phone lock apps (e.g., Forest, Focus Mode)
✓ Dedicated study playlists (lo-fi beats, ambient focus)

Create a **study sanctuary** that keeps your brain in learning mode.

3.4 Prioritize High-Yield Content

Here's where to focus based on previous exams and industry data:

Series 6	Series 63
Suitability scenarios	Fiduciary duty and unethical practices
Mutual fund share classes	Registration exemptions
Variable annuity fees & charges	Agent vs. broker-dealer distinctions
Customer profile & recommendation	Administrative penalties and actions

Don't waste energy mastering obscure facts that might not appear on your test.

3.5 Handle Test Anxiety with Rehearsal

If test anxiety is an issue:

✓ Meditate before study sessions
✓ Practice positive self-talk (e.g., "I am prepared, I know this.")
✓ Simulate test-day conditions (quiet room, timed practice)

Test confidence comes from familiarity. The more you rehearse, the calmer you'll be.

3.6 Use "Spaced Repetition"

Rather than rereading material over and over, space your review out over time. Example:

✓ Day 1: Learn
✓ Day 3: Review
✓ Day 6: Quiz
✓ Day 10: Reinforce

Apps like Anki or Brainscape are perfect for this technique.

3.7 Plan for Buffer Time

Life happens. Build in at least one buffer week before your scheduled test date. Use this for:

✓ Full-length simulations
✓ Weak spot reinforcement
✓ Rest and recharge

Never schedule your exam the day after a long trip, major event, or during personal stress.

CONCLUSION: STUDY SMARTER, NOT JUST HARDER

Success on the **Series 6 and 63 exams** isn't about raw hours—it's about **strategy**. This chapter has armed you with:

✓ A blueprint for creating your custom study plan
✓ High-quality, proven prep materials
✓ Time management tools to keep you focused and consistent

In the next chapter, we'll begin your deep dive into **actual exam content**, starting with the Series 6's Function 1: *Seeking Business for the Broker-Dealer*—one of the most practical and often misunderstood areas of the test.

CHAPTER 4
SEEKING BUSINESS FOR THE BROKER-DEALER

The first function tested on the Series 6 exam is foundational to everything a representative does: seeking business for the broker-dealer. Before you can recommend mutual funds, open accounts, or execute transactions, you must first attract prospects, establish relationships, and position your firm's services ethically and effectively.

This chapter will equip you to:
- ✓ Understand prospecting and marketing strategies allowed under regulatory rules
- ✓ Learn the fundamentals of investment company products you'll be promoting
- ✓ Stay compliant with strict FINRA and SEC communication standards

Whether you're working in a call center, meeting clients face-to-face, or marketing through digital media, everything begins with this essential phase.

SECTION 1: PROSPECTING AND MARKETING STRATEGIES

1.1 What Is Prospecting?

Prospecting is the process of identifying and engaging potential clients who may have a financial need or interest in your services. It's the first stage in the sales funnel, and it sets the tone for all future client interactions.

A successful Series 6 representative must:
✓ Know who to approach (ideal client profiles)
✓ Understand how to open conversations
✓ Adhere to compliance rules governing solicitation

1.2 Sources of Prospects

Source	Advantages	Considerations
Cold Calling	Broad reach, low cost	Must follow Telephone Consumer Protection Act (TCPA)
Referrals	High trust factor	Requires existing happy clients
Walk-ins	Natural interest already exists	Less predictable, requires availability
Social Media	Scalable and targeted outreach	Must follow FINRA rules on electronic communication
Networking Events	Build long-term business relationships	Time-intensive and not always scalable
Lead Services	Outsourced prospect generation	Costly and often impersonal

FINRA Rule 3230 governs outbound calling: No cold calls before 8 a.m. or after 9 p.m. in the client's time zone. You must maintain a **Do Not Call list** and provide a **firm name, your name, and contact information**.

1.3 Establishing Rapport and Qualification

Effective prospecting doesn't just mean reaching out—it means qualifying. This involves evaluating:

✓ Client's investment experience
✓ Financial goals and time horizons
✓ Risk tolerance
✓ Current holdings

This is the foundation of suitability, which will come into play in Chapter 6.

Sample opening questions:
✓ "What financial goals are you currently working toward?"
✓ "Are you currently investing through a retirement plan or brokerage?"
✓ "How comfortable are you with short-term risk in exchange for potential long-term growth?"

1.4 Marketing Channels and Compliance

Representatives must understand the difference between retail communication, correspondence, and institutional communication:

Type	Audience	Examples	FINRA Rule
Retail Communication	More than 25 retail clients	Social media ads, brochures	Rule 2210
Correspondence	25 or fewer retail clients	Personal emails, 1-on-1 letters	Rule 3110
Institutional Communication	Only institutional clients	Fund performance reports	Rule 2210

Any retail communication generally requires pre-approval by a principal. All communications must be:

✓ Fair and balanced
✓ Not misleading
✓ Include appropriate disclosures (e.g., "Past performance is not indicative of future results")

1.5 Email and Social Media Guidelines

Under FINRA rules:

✓ Firm approval is required for most advertisements and public posts
✓ Personal email use for business purposes is prohibited unless archived and monitored
✓ Testimonials (e.g., client reviews on Facebook) are allowed under strict conditions, but cannot imply endorsement of investment returns

1.6 Ethics in Marketing

Even before an account is opened, ethics matter. You cannot:

✓ Exaggerate returns ("We can double your money in 6 months!")
✓ Omit risks ("This fund is completely safe.")
✓ Use scare tactics ("You'll be broke without this annuity.")

These behaviors could trigger FINRA or SEC sanctions and lead to exam failure if demonstrated in a scenario-based question.

SECTION 2: UNDERSTANDING INVESTMENT COMPANY PRODUCTS

The products covered by the Series 6 license fall under **investment companies** as defined in the Investment Company Act of 1940.

2.1 Open-End vs. Closed-End Funds

Type	Open-End (Mutual Fund)	Closed-End
Shares Issued	Continuous	One-time IPO
Trading	Redeemable at NAV with issuer	Traded on exchanges like stocks
Pricing	Priced once daily (NAV + sales load)	Market price (may be at premium/discount)
Liquidity	Highly liquid	Depends on market activity

Mutual funds are the **core product** tested on Series 6. Closed-end funds may appear in comparative scenarios.

2.2 Mutual Fund Structure

Key terms to know:

- ✓ NAV (Net Asset Value): The price per share, calculated at market close
- ✓ POP (Public Offering Price): NAV + sales charge
- ✓ Sales Charge (Load): Commission paid to the broker-dealer, varies by share class
- ✓ 12b-1 Fees: Ongoing marketing/distribution fees
- ✓ Breakpoints: Volume discounts on sales charges for larger investments

2.3 Share Classes and Suitability

Class A	**Front-end load, lower annual fees — good for long-term investors**
Class B	Back-end (contingent deferred) load, converts to A — not good for short-term investors
Class C	Level load, higher annual fees — best for shorter time horizons

You must understand how to match the right class to the right investor, considering time horizon, investment size, and liquidity needs.

2.4 Variable Annuities and Insurance Products

Another major product category under Series 6:

- ✓ Variable annuities: Tax-deferred retirement vehicles with separate account investments
- ✓ Variable life insurance: Combines death benefit with investment options

Suitability and disclosure requirements are strict:
✓ Must disclose mortality and expense (M&E) charges
✓ Highlight surrender charges
✓ Explain subaccount performance volatility

2.5 Unit Investment Trusts (UITs)
✓ Fixed portfolio
✓ Not actively managed
✓ Often used for tax-sensitive investors

These rarely appear as the primary focus on the exam, but may be included in comparative product questions.

SECTION 3: REGULATORY CONSIDERATIONS
3.1 FINRA Rule 2210 – Communications with the Public

This rule governs all:
✓ Advertisements
✓ Sales literature
✓ Digital communication

Key principles:
✓ Must be fair and balanced
✓ Cannot predict or project performance
✓ Must prominently disclose risks and fees

3.2 SEC Rules on Prospectuses
Under Securities Act of 1933, mutual funds must provide a statutory prospectus prior to or at the time of sale.

A summary prospectus can be used if:
✓ The full version is available online
✓ Investors are given notice of their right to request the full version

3.3 Anti-Fraud and Suitability

Before you even make a sale, you're responsible for **accurate representations** and **suitability** assessment. Violations include:

✓ Omitting material facts
✓ Cherry-picking fund performance
✓ Misrepresenting past returns

Remember: even prospecting is subject to **FINRA and SEC review**.

3.4 Recordkeeping Requirements

All marketing communications must be retained for **three years** (per SEC Rule 17a-4). The first two years must be **easily accessible**. Firms typically archive:

✓ Emails
✓ Social media posts
✓ Marketing flyers
✓ Web advertisements

3.5 Common Violations to Avoid

Violation	Example
Misleading language	"This fund has never lost money."
Improper testimonials	"Look at my client's amazing results!"
Omission of disclosures	Failing to mention surrender periods
Hypothetical performance	Projecting what a fund *might* do

3.6 Handling Complaints at the Prospecting Stage

If a prospect expresses dissatisfaction or concern, even **before they become a client**, it must be treated as a **complaint** if it involves:

- ✓ Alleged misrepresentation
- ✓ Pressure to buy
- ✓ Rudeness or negligence

Such complaints must be reported to compliance and documented.

CONCLUSION: THE FIRST STEP TO A COMPLIANT CAREER

The ability to **seek business effectively and ethically** is what separates a qualified representative from a liability. In this chapter, you've learned:

- ✓ How to find and qualify prospects
- ✓ What types of communications are allowed
- ✓ Which products are included under your license
- ✓ How to stay compliant at every touch point

In the next chapter, we'll explore what happens once a prospect says "yes"—*Opening Customer Accounts*. This is where legal documentation, KYC rules, and client profiling come into full effect.

CHAPTER 5
OPENING CUSTOMER ACCOUNTS

Once a prospect agrees to become a client, the next critical step is opening their account — a process governed by **rigorous rules, documentation requirements, and ethical obligations**. This chapter focuses on the procedures, considerations, and regulatory guidelines that a registered representative must follow to open and maintain customer accounts properly.

We will cover:
✓ How to gather essential client information
✓ The importance of suitability and KYC (Know Your Customer) rules
✓ Types of account registrations and when to use them

Opening an account is more than data entry — it's the foundation of a long-term relationship built on compliance, suitability, and trust.

SECTION 1: GATHERING CLIENT INFORMATION

1.1 Regulatory Basis for Information Collection

Both **FINRA Rule 2090 (KYC Rule)** and **Rule 4512 (Customer Account Information)** mandate that broker-dealers **know essential facts about each customer** and their account.

This includes:
✓ The customer's financial profile
✓ Their investment objectives
✓ Their risk tolerance and time horizon
✓ Who is authorized to act on the account

These facts are used not only to determine **suitability** (see Chapter 6), but also to **prevent fraud**, **detect money laundering**, and **ensure proper recordkeeping**.

1.2 Minimum Required Information for a New Account

When opening any customer account, the firm must collect and maintain the following:

Information Required	Purpose
Customer's full legal name	Identity verification
Residential or business address	Communication and legal jurisdiction
Date of birth	Verify legal age to invest
Social Security number or Tax ID	IRS reporting and anti-money laundering
Occupation and employer	Assess income, risk, and conflicts of interest
Citizenship status	U.S. or foreign — may trigger additional disclosures
Marital status and dependents	Helps assess suitability and financial obligations
Financial information	Net worth, liquid net worth, income, tax bracket
Investment objectives	Growth, income, preservation of capital, speculation
Risk tolerance	Conservative, moderate, aggressive
Time horizon	Short, medium, long — informs product selection

1.3 Additional Considerations for FINRA and AML

In addition to KYC, representatives must comply with:

✓ Anti-Money Laundering (AML) policies under the Bank Secrecy Act
✓ Office of Foreign Assets Control (OFAC) checks
✓ USA PATRIOT Act requirements

Accounts must be checked against **terrorist watchlists**, **sanctioned nations**, and **suspicious activity patterns**.

Example: A U.S.-based client making frequent wire transfers to an unstable foreign country might trigger an SAR (Suspicious Activity Report) internally.

1.4 Account Approval Process

After information is collected, the process continues with:

1. Review by the registered representative
2. Principal approval — A principal of the firm must sign off on the new account before any trades occur
3. Creation of the customer profile within the firm's CRM or trading platform

Failure to obtain principal approval can lead to disciplinary actions or invalid trades.

SECTION 2: SUITABILITY AND KNOW-YOUR-CUSTOMER (KYC) RULES

2.1 FINRA Rule 2111 – Suitability Rule

Before recommending any investment, you must ensure it is **suitable** based on the client's:

✓ Investment profile
✓ Financial situation
✓ Experience and understanding
✓ Tax considerations

Three main types of suitability obligations apply:

Type of Suitability	Description
Reasonable-Basis	Is the investment generally suitable for anyone?
Customer-Specific	Is the investment suitable for this particular client?
Quantitative	Are there too many transactions that may indicate churning?

Matching investment options to risk tolerance is critical. Recommending a high-volatility fund to a conservative retiree could be considered unsuitable and trigger disciplinary action.

2.2 Documenting Suitability

Each recommendation must be documented and justified in the client's file. This may include:

✓ Fund comparison reports
✓ Risk disclosures
✓ Notes from the sales meeting or call

Firms often use automated systems to log suitability matches before allowing trades to proceed.

2.3 Ongoing Review and Updates

KYC is not a one-time task. It must be:

✓ Updated at least every 36 months
✓ Reviewed whenever there is a material change in the client's profile (e.g., divorce, retirement, large inheritance)

You are expected to know when these updates are necessary and ensure they are carried out.

SECTION 3: ACCOUNT REGISTRATION TYPES

3.1 Individual Accounts

✓ Owned by a single person
✓ That person has full authority
✓ Upon death, assets typically go through probate

3.2 Joint Accounts

Shared by two or more people. The two primary types are:

Type	Features
Joint Tenants with Right of Survivorship (JTWROS)	Equal ownership; surviving tenant automatically inherits assets
Tenants in Common (TIC)	Unequal ownership allowed; decedent's share goes to their estate

JTWROS is common for spouses; TIC is often used in business relationships.

3.3 Corporate and Institutional Accounts

✓ Require corporate resolution authorizing account opening
✓ May require charter documents
✓ Must designate an authorized individual or officer

3.4 Custodial Accounts (UGMA/UTMA)

Used for minors:

✓ Assets managed by a custodian until the child reaches the age of majority
✓ Contributions are irrevocable
✓ Tax implications vary by state

Used to teach investing or save for college, these are often referenced in Series 6 suitability scenarios.

3.5 Retirement Accounts

Account Type	Features
Traditional IRA	Tax-deferred; contributions may be deductible
Roth IRA	After-tax contributions; tax-free withdrawals
403(b)/401(k)	Employer-sponsored; pre-tax contributions

While opening these accounts often involves third-party custodians, representatives must understand the basics, especially regarding rollovers, beneficiary designations, and early withdrawal penalties.

3.6 Trust Accounts

Trusts require:

✓ Trust agreement documentation
✓ Trustee authorization
✓ Special care in understanding grantor vs. irrevocable trusts

They may have specific investment restrictions, which must be observed. Failing to respect a trust's investment objectives can lead to liability.

3.7 Margin vs. Cash Accounts *(Series 6 Limited Scope)*

While Series 6 reps generally do not open margin accounts, it's important to understand the difference:

✓ Cash Account: Client pays in full for securities
✓ Margin Account: Client borrows money to purchase securities (Series 7 license required)

You should know that mutual funds and UITs cannot be bought on margin.

3.8 Account Transfers

Accounts can be transferred from one broker-dealer to another using the Automated Customer Account Transfer Service (ACATS). During transfer:

✓ Open orders must be canceled
✓ Assets are frozen
✓ Transfer typically completes in 3–5 business days

Representatives must clearly communicate this process and timing to clients.

SECTION 4: REGULATORY FORMS AND DISCLOSURES

4.1 New Account Form (NAF)

The cornerstone document that includes:

✓ Personal identification info
✓ Employment and financial data
✓ Investment objectives
✓ Risk tolerance

Must be reviewed by a **designated principal**.

4.2 Form U4

Used to register a representative with:

✓ FINRA
✓ State regulators

Not client-facing, but every rep must know that false information on Form U4 is grounds for disqualification.

4.3 Customer Account Agreement

Outlines terms of service, arbitration clauses, and:

✓ Trading authorizations
✓ Communication preferences
✓ Beneficiary designations

4.4 Privacy Disclosures (Reg S-P)

Firms must provide:

✓ Initial and annual privacy notices
✓ Clear opt-out mechanisms if personal information is shared with affiliates

Failure to do so violates SEC privacy rules.

4.5 Business Continuity and SIPC Disclosures

✓ Customers must be informed of how the firm will operate in emergencies
✓ SIPC membership and insurance coverage must be disclosed upon account opening

Conclusion: Building Trust with Every New Account

Opening a customer account is far more than filling in forms — it's about:

✓ Understanding the client
✓ Complying with regulations
✓ Documenting accurately
✓ Setting the foundation for suitability and ethical service

Every recommendation and transaction begins here. Your ability to gather accurate information and apply it responsibly will be critical to your success — both on the exam and in your career.

In the next chapter, we'll explore the heart of Series 6 advising: **Providing Investment Information and Recommendations.**

CHAPTER 6
PROVIDING INVESTMENT INFORMATION AND RECOMMENDATIONS

Once an account is opened, the Series 6 representative shifts from discovery and documentation to **recommendation** — helping clients make informed investment decisions. This is where theoretical knowledge must translate into real-world guidance, and where ethics and compliance meet sales and service.

This chapter builds your understanding of:

✓ The investment products you're licensed to offer

✓ How to match product features with client needs and profiles

✓ The role of risk and return, and how to communicate it

✓ The importance of ethical sales practices and avoiding prohibited behaviors

Whether you're recommending a mutual fund for retirement or a variable annuity for long-term income, your ability to inform clients accurately and recommend responsibly will define your professional credibility.

SECTION 1: UNDERSTANDING MUTUAL FUNDS AND VARIABLE CONTRACTS

1.1 What Are Mutual Funds?

A mutual fund is a professionally managed investment pool that collects money from many investors and invests it in a diversified portfolio of stocks, bonds, or other securities. These are structured as open-end investment companies under the Investment Company Act of 1940.

Key features:

✓ Diversification: Spread risk across multiple securities
✓ Liquidity: Shares can be redeemed at the end of each business day at NAV
✓ Professional management: Fund managers make allocation decisions
✓ Affordability: Low initial investment thresholds
✓ Regulation: Subject to SEC and FINRA rules

1.2 Key Mutual Fund Concepts

Term	Definition
Net Asset Value (NAV)	Total assets minus liabilities, divided by shares outstanding
Public Offering Price (POP)	NAV plus the sales charge (applicable to Class A shares)
Expense Ratio	Annual fund operating expenses as a percentage of assets
12b-1 Fees	Annual marketing/distribution fees deducted from fund assets
Load vs. No-Load	Load funds have sales charges; no-load funds do not
Breakpoints	Discounts on sales charges based on investment size (Class A only)

Rights of Accumulation	Combine new purchases with previous holdings to qualify for breakpoints
Letter of Intent (LOI)	Investor agrees to invest a certain amount over 13 months to qualify for breakpoints

1.3 Share Classes and Suitability

Different mutual fund share classes carry different fee structures, influencing their suitability:

Class A	Front-end load, lower ongoing fees; ideal for long-term investors
Class B	Back-end load (CDSC), higher fees; converts to Class A eventually
Class C	Level load; no front/back loads, but higher annual fees

Recommending the wrong share class for a client's time horizon could be a sales practice violation.

1.4 Variable Annuities (VAs)

A variable annuity is a contract between an investor and an insurance company that provides:

✓ Tax-deferred growth
✓ Investment choices via subaccounts
✓ Optional riders like guaranteed income or death benefits

Key characteristics:

✓ Funded with after-tax dollars
✓ Earnings grow tax-deferred
✓ Subject to surrender charges for early withdrawal
✓ May offer living benefits (e.g., guaranteed minimum income)

Suitability considerations:

✓ Long-term investment horizon
✓ Clients with maxed-out 401(k)/IRA contributions
✓ Willingness to pay higher fees for guarantees

1.5 Variable Life Insurance

Like VAs, variable life insurance offers investment options but adds a death benefit. Premiums are fixed or flexible. The cash value fluctuates based on the performance of subaccounts.

Must disclose:

✓ Investment risk
✓ M&E expenses
✓ Possible loss of principal

1.6 Unit Investment Trusts (UITs)

A UIT is a fixed portfolio of securities with a predetermined life. Not actively managed. Typically invests in:

✓ Municipal bonds
✓ Corporate bonds
✓ Equities

UITs are redeemable securities and may be suitable for conservative clients seeking predictable income.

SECTION 2: UNDERSTANDING RISK AND RETURN

2.1 The Risk-Return Tradeoff

All investments involve risk. The higher the **potential return**, the higher the **potential risk**. Your role is to ensure clients understand this balance.

Risk Type	Description
Market Risk	Risk of overall market decline
Interest Rate Risk	Bonds lose value when rates rise
Credit Risk	Issuer may default on obligations
Inflation Risk	Purchasing power eroded over time

Liquidity Risk	Difficulty selling without loss of value
Political/Regulatory Risk	Laws or government actions affect performance
Investment-Specific Risk	Poor management or performance by a single fund or company

2.2 Risk Profiling Clients

You must assess risk tolerance during account setup:

✓ Age
✓ Income
✓ Net worth
✓ Investment experience
✓ Time horizon

You can use risk tolerance questionnaires to categorize clients as:
✓ Conservative
✓ Moderate
✓ Aggressive

2.3 Types of Returns

Return Type	Calculation or Impact
Total Return	Income + capital gains / beginning value
Real Return	Total return adjusted for inflation
Tax-Equivalent Return	Compares tax-free and taxable bonds (used for muni bond comparisons)
Yield	Income as a % of current price (used for bonds)

Variable annuity returns are taxed as **ordinary income**, not capital gains.

2.4 Measuring Risk and Return: Key Metrics

Metric	Definition
Standard Deviation	Measures volatility
Sharpe Ratio	Return vs. risk (higher = better risk-adjusted return)
Beta	Measures movement vs. market; beta > 1 = more volatile
Alpha	Measures performance above benchmark
R-Squared	Correlation with benchmark performance

SECTION 3: SALES PRACTICES AND ETHICAL CONSIDERATIONS

3.1 FINRA Suitability Rule (Rule 2111)

Suitability is not optional. It's the core compliance obligation of any recommendation.

You must:
✓ Have reasonable basis for the investment
✓ Ensure it's appropriate for this specific customer
✓ Avoid excessive trading or "churning"

3.2 The Disclosure Principle

Clients must be given **complete and accurate information** before making a decision.

Required disclosures include:
✓ Fees (front-end/back-end loads, 12b-1)
✓ Risks (market volatility, liquidity)
✓ Charges (surrender charges in annuities)
✓ Investment objectives

3.3 Prohibited Sales Practices

Violation	Example
Misrepresentation	"This fund guarantees 12% annual returns"
Omission of Material Fact	Failing to disclose surrender charges on a VA
Exaggeration	"This fund is recession-proof"
Unsuitable Recommendation	Recommending Class B shares to a short-term investor
Breakpoint Sale Abuse	Splitting a $50,000 investment into smaller parts to avoid discounts
Switching Abuse	Moving from one fund to another without justification

3.4 The Role of Written Supervisory Procedures (WSPs)

Firms create internal WSPs to:

✓ Monitor representative activity
✓ Ensure compliance with FINRA/SEC regulations
✓ Document supervisory review of recommendations

As a rep, you're expected to:
✓ Understand your firm's WSPs
✓ Seek supervisory approval when needed
✓ Document your rationale for each recommendation

3.5 Customer Complaints and Reporting

A complaint must be documented if:

✓ It's written
✓ It alleges sales practice violations

All written complaints must be:

✓ Reported to FINRA
✓ Logged and reviewed by a principal
✓ Responded to within firm timelines

3.6 Maintaining Records

Firms must retain records of:

✓ All communications
✓ Product disclosures
✓ Signed suitability assessments
✓ Transaction records

Retention periods vary, but most customer documents must be retained for three years, with two years easily accessible.

SECTION 4: REAL-WORLD SCENARIOS AND PRACTICE CASES

4.1 Scenario: Retiree Investing an Inheritance

Client: 68-year-old retired school teacher
Goal: Preserve capital, generate income
Recommendation: Balanced mutual fund with moderate bond allocation
Suitable? Yes
Avoid: Variable annuity with high fees or aggressive growth fund

4.2 Scenario: 35-Year-Old with Long Time Horizon

Client: Software engineer saving for retirement in 25 years
Goal: Growth with long-term horizon
Recommendation: Equity-focused mutual fund or variable annuity with growth-oriented subaccounts
Suitable? Yes
Avoid: Class A shares if investing under $1,000 (due to sales load inefficiency)

4.3 Scenario: Widow Needs Guaranteed Income

Client: 62-year-old widow, no pension, needs guaranteed income

Goal: Supplement Social Security

Recommendation: Variable annuity with guaranteed lifetime income rider

Suitable? Yes — explain fees clearly

Avoid: Recommending without proper insurance license

4.4 Scenario: Young Investor with Low Risk Tolerance

Client: 25-year-old, new to investing, conservative mindset

Goal: Preservation of capital

Recommendation: Conservative mutual fund or fixed annuity (if available)

Suitable? Yes

Avoid: Small-cap or tech-focused funds without educating on risk

CONCLUSION: RECOMMENDING WITH RESPONSIBILITY

This chapter covered what is arguably the heart of the Series 6 representative's role — not just selling, but informing, matching, and acting ethically.

You now understand:

✓ The structure, benefits, and risks of mutual funds, variable annuities, and other Series 6 products

✓ The importance of aligning investment recommendations with each client's profile

✓ How to navigate compliance, documentation, and ethical requirements with confidence

In the next chapter, we'll complete the client lifecycle with Processing and Confirming Transactions — the final phase where recommendations are executed and legally confirmed.

CHAPTER 7
PROCESSING AND CONFIRMING TRANSACTIONS

All the research, relationship-building, and recommendations culminate in a simple but high-stakes moment: **executing the transaction**. This chapter covers the life cycle of a trade—from order entry to confirmation, settlement, and record retention.

Whether you're processing mutual fund purchases, variable annuity applications, or handling fund switches, you are responsible for:

✓ Accurately entering client instructions
✓ Ensuring timely execution
✓ Providing prompt confirmations
✓ Complying with regulatory settlement timelines
✓ Maintaining records for supervision and auditing

This chapter focuses on what happens **after the recommendation**—when the client says "yes." That's when the rules become more technical, and **errors become liabilities**.

SECTION 1: ORDER ENTRY AND EXECUTION

1.1 Capturing the Client's Intent

Every order begins with a client's **instruction**—which must be clear, complete, and properly documented. You cannot make assumptions or take discretion unless authorized.

You must record:

✓ The security/product requested
✓ The action (buy, sell, exchange)
✓ The quantity or dollar amount
✓ Any special instructions (e.g., reinvest dividends)
✓ The time the instruction was given

Example: A client calls to purchase $5,000 of ABC Growth Mutual Fund. You must note the exact time of the call and details of the order.

1.2 Authorized Parties

Only authorized account holders or authorized agents (such as power of attorney or trustee) can place orders. Accepting instructions from an unauthorized person—even a spouse—can constitute a serious violation.

Allowed: Client's legal guardian places an order on a UTMA account.
Not allowed: Client's friend calls in with instructions.

1.3 No Discretion Unless Written Authorization

Unless you have **written discretionary authority**, you must not:

✓ Decide what to buy or sell
✓ Choose how much to invest
✓ Time the trade

Discretionary authority must be:
✓ Signed by the client
✓ Reviewed and approved by a principal
✓ Logged and regularly reviewed

1.4 Processing Mutual Fund Orders

Unlike stocks, mutual fund shares do not trade intraday. Instead:

✓ Orders are executed at the next computed NAV (typically after 4 p.m. EST)
✓ This is called forward pricing, mandated by the Investment Company Act of 1940

If a client submits an order at 3:59 p.m., they receive **today's NAV**
If submitted at 4:01 p.m., the order is processed at **tomorrow's NAV**

1.5 Settlement Dates and Timelines

Product	Settlement Rule
Mutual funds	T+1 (trade date + 1 business day)
UITs and primary issues	Varies; usually T+2
Variable annuities	Can be delayed due to underwriting
Retirement accounts	May require custodial processing

T+1 means if a trade occurs on Monday, it settles Tuesday.

Settlement must occur on time unless:
✓ The firm extends credit (which Series 6 reps cannot do)
✓ There's a documented issue requiring extension

1.6 Canceling or Correcting Trades

You may cancel or correct a trade if:

✓ It was entered in error
✓ The client changes their mind before the trade is executed
✓ A processing error occurred (e.g., transposed account number)

Corrections must be:
✓ Reported to a supervisor
✓ Fully documented
✓ Approved by a principal

Never backdate or delete trade entries. Doing so is a violation of **SEC Rule 17a-4**.

SECTION 2: TRADE CONFIRMATIONS AND CLIENT NOTIFICATIONS

2.1 The Confirmation Requirement

Per **SEC Rule 10b-10**, customers must receive **a written confirmation** of their transaction **at or before settlement**. The confirmation includes:

Item	Details Provided
Security name	Full fund name, including share class
Action	Buy, sell, exchange
Dollar amount or share quantity	Amount invested, number of shares bought
Price and NAV	NAV at trade time, sales load if applicable
Fees and charges	Commissions, 12b-1 fees, surrender charges
Account number	Customer's account ID
Date and time of transaction	Time-stamp of the order
Settlement date	When funds/securities must exchange hands

2.2 Disclosures in Confirmations

The confirmation may also include:

✓ Statement that the investment is not FDIC insured
✓ No guarantee of principal (unless it's a guaranteed product)
✓ Risk disclosures for variable products

These disclosures protect the firm and clarify the **nature of the investment**.

2.3 Confirming Variable Annuity Transactions

VAs often require **separate confirmation documents**, including:

✓ Insurance company acknowledgment
✓ Subaccount allocation
✓ M&E fees
✓ Surrender schedule

Because VAs are insurance and securities products, they are subject to dual regulation (FINRA + state insurance department).

2.4 Client Communications after Trades

It is good practice to:

✓ Follow up with a thank-you call or email
✓ Offer to answer any follow-up questions
✓ Remind the client about performance monitoring

This builds trust and helps identify misunderstandings before they escalate.

2.5 Reversals and Adjustments

If a client disputes a trade, the rep must:

✓ Report the issue to a supervisor immediately
✓ Document the concern
✓ Avoid making unauthorized promises

If the firm finds the dispute valid, a reversal or adjustment may be issued. These actions must be logged and audited regularly.

SECTION 3: RECORDKEEPING AND COMPLIANCE REQUIREMENTS

3.1 Why Recordkeeping Matters

Recordkeeping is not optional—it's a legal obligation. FINRA, SEC, and NASAA require broker-dealers to retain records of:

✓ Transactions
✓ Customer communications
✓ Confirmations
✓ Complaints
✓ Disclosures
✓ Recommendations
✓ Approvals and supervisory reviews

Records must be:
✓ Accurate
✓ Accessible
✓ Secure from tampering

3.2 Required Retention Periods

Document Type	Retention Timeframe
Trade confirmations	3 years
Customer account records	6 years
Account opening forms (NAF, LOI)	6 years
Email and electronic communication	3 years (2 years easily accessible)
Written complaints	4 years

SEC Rule 17a-4 and **FINRA Rule 4511** govern these timelines.

3.3 Supervisory Review Logs

Each trade or recommendation must be reviewed by a **designated principal**. The principal ensures:

✓ Suitability has been assessed
✓ Required disclosures were made
✓ Fees and charges are appropriate
✓ The rep is acting within their license

These logs are also reviewed during **regulatory audits**.

3.4 Communications and Archiving

All written communications (email, letters, texts, even social media messages) related to securities business must be archived and reviewed periodically.

Firms typically:
✓ Use automated systems to detect red flags
✓ Flag communications containing phrases like "guaranteed return" or "risk-free"
✓ Require supervisory sign-off on all marketing pieces before use

3.5 Trade Blotters and Order Tickets

A trade blotter is a chronological record of all trades. It helps regulators:

✓ Reconstruct events
✓ Identify patterns (e.g., churning or excessive trades)

Order tickets contain:
✓ Rep ID
✓ Client account

✓ Security details
✓ Time and method of order receipt

Missing or falsified order tickets = **major compliance violation**.

3.6 Exceptions and Corrections

✓ Errors must be documented and corrected promptly. Key rules:
✓ Don't conceal errors from clients or supervisors
✓ File a corrective ticket and label as "Error"
✓ Submit to compliance for final review
✓ Never use personal funds to "make it right" — this could be considered selling away

SECTION 4: TRANSACTION TYPES AND THEIR REQUIREMENTS

4.1 Purchases and Redemptions

Action	Rules
Purchase	Must match client's risk profile; executed at forward NAV
Redemption	Processed at next NAV; funds must be delivered within 7 calendar days

Firms must forward redemption requests to mutual fund companies same-day under FINRA Rule 2341.

4.2 Exchanges and Switches

An exchange is when a client moves money between funds within the same fund family.

A switch involves changing fund families—this:
✓ May trigger sales charges
✓ Requires a switch letter
✓ Must be justified as suitable and beneficial

Recommending switches to generate commissions = prohibited practice

4.3 Breakpoint Monitoring

Systems must detect when:

✓ A client is eligible for breakpoint discounts
✓ Multiple accounts under the same household apply
✓ Letters of Intent or Rights of Accumulation should be applied

Failure to apply breakpoints is a FINRA enforcement priority and often audited.

4.4 Reinvestment Options

Clients may opt to:
✓ Reinvest dividends into additional shares
✓ Receive dividends and capital gains as cash

This decision must be documented at account setup and confirmed on each statement.

4.5 Handling Delays and Outages

If a trading platform is down:

✓ Notify clients
✓ Escalate to a supervisor
✓ Document all communications

Under Regulation S-P, you must ensure data security, even during outages.

CONCLUSION: FROM ENTRY TO EXECUTION WITH PRECISION

Executing client instructions is more than a back-office task — it's the legal, financial, and ethical completion of your role as a registered rep.

You are now prepared to:

✓ Enter orders with confidence and accuracy

✓ Navigate settlement rules and confirmation requirements

✓ Comply with strict recordkeeping and supervision rules

✓ Recognize prohibited practices before they become violations

In the next chapter, we shift focus from the Series 6 to the **Series 63**, beginning with State Securities Acts and Related Rules. Get ready to explore the legal side of the industry and understand your obligations at the state level.

CHAPTER 8
STATE SECURITIES ACTS AND RELATED RULES

While the Series 6 focuses on federal regulations and product-based licensing, the Series 63 brings you face to face with the state-level laws that govern your right to do business as a securities agent. No matter how qualified or experienced you are, you cannot legally operate in most states without satisfying the rules of that state's securities authority.

This chapter introduces the Uniform Securities Act (USA)—the model law adopted (with variations) by most states. You'll learn how the USA defines securities, regulates registrations, and empowers state administrators. You'll also explore exemptions, broker-dealer and agent registration, and the key legal distinctions every representative must know.

SECTION 1: OVERVIEW OF THE UNIFORM SECURITIES ACT (USA)

1.1 What Is the USA?

The **Uniform Securities Act (USA)** is a model law developed by the North American Securities Administrators Association (NASAA) to guide state legislatures in crafting their own securities laws. It is not federal law, but most U.S. states and territories have adopted it in some form.

Purpose of the USA:
✓ Protect investors from fraudulent practices
✓ Ensure full disclosure in securities transactions
✓ Define clear standards for the registration of securities, firms, and agents
✓ Grant enforcement powers to state securities administrators

While the SEC governs interstate and federal securities, the USA governs intrastate (within-state) transactions and provides tools for enforcement.

1.2 Role of the State Securities Administrator

Each state appoints a **Securities Administrator**—typically the Commissioner of Securities or an agency director—with broad powers, including:

Power	Function
Issue rules and orders	Clarify or modify the USA as applied in that state
Conduct investigations	Even across state lines and without advance notice
Subpoena witnesses and documents	Compel cooperation during investigations
Enforce cease-and-desist orders	Halt fraudulent or illegal activities immediately
Deny, suspend, revoke registration	Take administrative action against registrants

Administrators can act proactively, even if no formal complaint has been filed.

1.3 What Is a "Security" Under the USA?

The USA defines **securities broadly**, covering traditional and nontraditional products.

Examples of securities:
✓ Stocks, bonds, notes
✓ Options, futures, puts/calls

✓ Variable annuities
✓ Investment contracts (including schemes like real estate limited partnerships)

Non-securities (not regulated under the USA):
✓ Fixed annuities
✓ Whole life insurance
✓ Collectibles
✓ Commodities and futures contracts (not the options on them)

The Howey Test is often used to define a security:
An investment of money in a common enterprise with an expectation of profits from the efforts of others.

SECTION 2: REGISTRATION OF SECURITIES

2.1 Who Must Register Securities?

Under the USA, any **issuer** offering securities in a state must either:

✓ Register the securities, or
✓ Qualify for an exemption

Issuers may include corporations, partnerships, or even governments.

2.2 Methods of Registration

There are three ways to register securities at the state level:

Method	Used When	Key Features
Registration by Notification	For established, well-known companies	Fastest method; minimal disclosures; used for blue-chip issuers
Registration by Coordination	When also registering federally (with SEC)	File simultaneously with SEC and state

Registration by Qualification	Intrastate offerings or when not using SEC registration	Most detailed and burdensome; full disclosure required

Test Tip: Coordination = SEC + state. Qualification = state only.

2.3 Effective Dates and Amendments

✓ Registration becomes effective at a specified time or when approved by the administrator.

✓ If information in the registration becomes outdated or materially incorrect, amendments must be filed.

✓ Registrations are effective for one year from the effective date.

2.4 Prospectus Delivery and Fraud Prevention

Issuers must:

✓ Provide full disclosure of material facts

✓ Deliver a prospectus or offering circular

✓ Avoid any false or misleading statements

Failure to do so is considered fraud, even if unintentional.

SECTION 3: EXEMPTIONS FROM REGISTRATION

3.1 Exempt Securities

Certain securities are exempt from state registration, often because they're considered low risk or already subject to other oversight.

Examples:

✓ U.S. government and agency securities

✓ Municipal bonds (unless offered to residents of the issuer's state)

✓ Securities issued by banks or credit unions

✓ Commercial paper (maturing in ≤ 270 days)

✓ Securities listed on national exchanges (NYSE, Nasdaq)

3.2 Exempt Transactions

Certain types of transactions are exempt, even if the securities themselves are not.

Type of Transaction	Explanation
Isolated nonissuer transactions	One-time resale by someone not affiliated with the issuer
Unsolicited transactions	Trades initiated by the client without rep recommendation
Fiduciary transactions	Trades by executors, trustees, or guardians
Private placements	Sales to ≤10 investors in 12 months, with no public solicitation

Most Series 63 questions test your ability to distinguish between exempt securities vs. exempt transactions.

3.3 Federal Covered Securities

These are securities **exempt from state registration altogether**, thanks to federal preemption.

They include:

✓ Securities listed on NYSE, Nasdaq
✓ Mutual fund shares
✓ Securities issued by registered investment companies
✓ Reg D private placements

While the state cannot require registration, they can:

✓ Require a notice filing
✓ Collect filing fees

SECTION 4: REGISTRATION OF BROKER-DEALERS AND AGENTS

4.1 Who Is a Broker-Dealer?

A broker-dealer (BD) is a firm engaged in:

✓ The business of effecting securities transactions
✓ For its own account or the accounts of others

Examples:
✓ Merrill Lynch
✓ Edward Jones
✓ Independent firms and online platforms

Not considered BDs under USA:
✓ Issuers (selling their own securities)
✓ Agents (individuals working for BDs)
✓ Banks, savings institutions, and trust companies
✓ Individuals trading for themselves (non-compensated)

4.2 Registration of BDs

To register in a state, a BD must:

✓ File Form BD
✓ Pay filing fees
✓ Consent to service of process
✓ Maintain net capital requirements
✓ Submit financial reports as required by the Administrator

BDs must also designate a supervisory principal, who is accountable for compliance.

4.3 Who Is an Agent?

An agent (also called a registered representative) is an individual who represents:

✓ A broker-dealer, or
✓ An issuer (in some cases)

Agents must register in each state where they:
✓ Solicit securities business
✓ Accept orders or provide investment recommendations

Even if you're licensed under FINRA (Series 6), you cannot legally do business in a state unless you're registered as an agent **under that state's laws**.

4.4 Agent Registration Requirements

Agents must:

✓ File Form U4 through their firm
✓ Pass a qualification exam (usually Series 63)
✓ Consent to criminal background and fingerprinting
✓ Receive approval from the Administrator

Registration becomes effective when:
✓ Approved by the Administrator
✓ The BD is also registered in that state

4.5 Termination and Renewal

If an agent leaves the firm:

✓ The firm files Form U5
✓ The Administrator is notified
✓ Registration is terminated

All registrations expire on December 31 each year and must be renewed annually, even if approved mid-year.

4.6 Dual Registration

An agent may not be registered with multiple BDs simultaneously in most states unless:

✓ The Administrator grants an exception
✓ The agent works under a common control arrangement

SECTION 5: LEGAL CONCEPTS AND ADMINISTRATOR POWERS

5.1 Administrator's Authority

Administrators can:

✓ Subpoena witnesses and documents
✓ Conduct on-site inspections
✓ Issue cease and desist orders
✓ Deny, suspend, or revoke registrations
✓ Refer cases to criminal courts

They may act without prior notice, especially when public interest is at stake.

5.2 Statutory Disqualification

Registrants may be disqualified for:

✓ Conviction of a securities- or money-related felony in the last 10 years
✓ Willful violations of the USA or SEC rules
✓ Making false or misleading statements on Form U4 or BD
✓ Failing to supervise subordinates

Administrators must provide:
✓ Notice of action
✓ Hearing opportunity
✓ Written findings

5.3 Recordkeeping Requirements

State laws may require BDs and agents to retain:

✓ Trade blotters
✓ Customer account records
✓ Complaints and correspondence
✓ Advertising materials

Firms must retain records for at least **3–6 years**, depending on the type.

5.4 Criminal vs. Civil Penalties

Type	Applies To	Penalties
Criminal	Willful violations, fraud	Fines up to $5,000, prison up to 3 years
Civil	Selling unregistered securities, unsuitable advice	Rescission offers, damages, interest

Conclusion: Know the Rules, Protect the Client, Protect Yourself

The Series 63 exists for a reason — state regulators are the final gatekeepers for client protection. By mastering the USA, you:

✓ Understand what can be sold in your state
✓ Know when registration is required—and when it's not
✓ Can confidently assess your own responsibilities and limitations

In the next chapter, we'll dive deeper into the ethical and fiduciary standards expected of all licensed agents.

CHAPTER 9:
ETHICAL PRACTICES AND FIDUCIARY OBLIGATIONS

Securities regulations don't exist merely to prevent crime—they exist to protect the core currency of the financial industry: trust. As a registered representative or agent, you are legally obligated to uphold the highest ethical standards. Even one dishonest recommendation, one conflict of interest, or one failure to disclose material information can trigger severe penalties and permanently damage your reputation.

This chapter focuses on what separates competent professionals from truly **trustworthy fiduciaries**:

✓ Ethical behavior and professional conduct
✓ Identifying and managing conflicts of interest
✓ Acting in the best interest of your client

SECTION 1: FRAUDULENT AND PROHIBITED PRACTICES

1.1 What Is Fraud?

Under both the Uniform Securities Act (USA) and federal law, fraud includes any intentional or negligent act of deception, misstatement, or omission of material facts made in connection with the offer or sale of a security.

Fraud does not require that the client suffer a financial loss — the mere act or intent is enough for enforcement.

1.2 Types of Fraudulent Activity

Type	Description
Misrepresentation	Making untrue statements (e.g., "This fund is guaranteed to double.")
Omission of Material Facts	Withholding critical details (e.g., failing to mention a surrender charge)
Churning	Excessive trading for the purpose of generating commissions
Unsuitable Recommendations	Making a recommendation inconsistent with the client's profile
Unauthorized Transactions	Executing a trade without the client's permission or discretion
Fictitious Accounts	Creating fake clients/accounts to inflate performance or collect bonuses
Front-Running	Executing a personal or firm trade in advance of a client order
Selling Away	Selling securities not approved or offered by your firm

Even "puffing" or exaggerating product benefits can be considered a violation.

1.3 Penalties for Fraud

Depending on severity and intent:

- Civil penalties may include restitution, interest, rescission, or administrative fines
- Criminal penalties (for willful violations) may include:
- Fines up to $5,000 per offense

- Up to 3 years imprisonment
- Permanent revocation of license

1.4 Red Flag Behaviors

As a rep, be vigilant for the following **common red flags** in colleague or competitor behavior:

- "All upside, no downside" pitches
- Frequent switching of mutual funds without reason
- Patterns of complaints or canceled trades
- Promising returns above the market rate with "no risk"

Report questionable behavior to your **supervisor** or **compliance officer** immediately.

SECTION 2: CONFLICTS OF INTEREST

2.1 What Is a Conflict of Interest?

A conflict of interest occurs when your professional judgment or recommendations could be compromised by personal, financial, or institutional incentives.

Conflicts don't always involve malicious intent — but if they are not disclosed and managed, they are unethical and often illegal.

2.2 Common Conflicts of Interest

Conflict	Example
Compensation-Based Bias	Recommending a fund that pays a higher commission, even if it's not the best fit
Gifts and Entertainment	Accepting lavish gifts from a wholesaler in exchange for promoting their fund

Outside Business Activities	Working for another firm or financial entity without disclosure
Personal Trading Conflicts	Trading the same securities as your client before entering their orders
Proprietary Product Preference	Recommending firm-sponsored funds without proper justification

2.3 Disclosure and Mitigation

The first step in handling a conflict of interest is full and prompt disclosure. Clients must:
✓ Know that the conflict exists
✓ Understand its nature
✓ Be given enough information to assess the recommendation fairly

Firms typically require:
✓ Written disclosures
✓ Client acknowledgment
✓ Supervisory review

Failure to disclose is grounds for disciplinary action, suspension, or termination.

2.4 Best Execution vs. Compensation

You are required to pursue best execution—getting the best price, speed, and service for your client's order—even if it means lower commissions or choosing a product with lower compensation.

You must always put the client's interest before your own.

SECTION 3: FIDUCIARY DUTY AND CLIENT COMMUNICATIONS

3.1 Fiduciary Standard vs. Suitability Standard

Under **state securities laws**, a representative is expected to act under a **fiduciary standard**—a legal obligation to act **solely in the client's best interest.**

Suitability Standard	Fiduciary Standard
Is the recommendation "good enough"?	Is this the **best** option for the client?
Reps can consider firm incentives	Must **ignore** personal or firm incentives
No duty to monitor after recommendation	Ongoing duty of care
Applies to Series 6 reps	Applies to **investment advisers and sometimes Series 63 reps**

3.2 Communication Best Practices

Clear communication is not just good service—it's a legal obligation.

All communications must be:
✓ Fair and balanced
✓ Free from exaggerated claims
✓ Not misleading or incomplete

Examples:
✓ Don't say: "This fund always performs well."
✓ Do say: "Historically, the fund has had strong returns, but past performance does not guarantee future results."

3.3 Types of Communications

Communication Type	Definition	Regulation
Retail Communication	≥25 retail clients within 30 days (e.g., brochures)	FINRA Rule 2210
Correspondence	≤25 retail clients (e.g., emails, letters)	FINRA Rule 3110
Institutional Communication	Sent to institutional investors only	Less strict, but still supervised

3.4 Supervision of Communication

All client-facing communications are subject to **supervisory review**, and most require:

✓ Pre-approval by a principal
✓ Archiving for 3 years
✓ Periodic compliance audits

This includes:
✓ Social media posts
✓ Email newsletters
✓ Client presentations
✓ Personal text messages related to firm business

3.5 Testimonials and Endorsements

Under NASAA and FINRA guidance:

✓ Testimonials must not be misleading
✓ Must disclose whether compensation was given
✓ Should not imply performance guarantees
✓ Often require firm review and approval

Example:
"My advisor is always responsive."
"My advisor helped me triple my money."

SECTION 4: OTHER KEY ETHICAL CONCEPTS AND SCENARIOS

4.1 Soft Dollars

"**Soft dollars**" are compensation arrangements between broker-dealers and investment advisers where the adviser receives **research or services** in exchange for directing client trades.

Rules:
✓ Must benefit the client (not the adviser personally)
✓ Must be disclosed
✓ Cannot be used for rent, travel, entertainment

4.2 Insider Trading

Using **material, nonpublic information** to trade securities is **illegal** under the **Securities Exchange Act of 1934**.

Both:
✓ The tipper (who provides the info), and
✓ The tippee (who trades on it)

...may be held liable.

Preventive Measures:
✓ Avoid discussing client or firm matters in public
✓ Report suspicious activity to your supervisor or compliance

4.3 Gifts and Gratuities

Under FINRA rules:

✓ Reps may not give or receive gifts over $100 per person per year
✓ Business entertainment is allowed if not excessive
✓ All gifts must be logged and reported

4.4 Political Contributions – Pay-to-Play Rules

The SEC restricts reps from doing business with municipalities if they've made political contributions to officials who influence hiring decisions.

✓ "Cooling off" period: 2 years
✓ Applies to municipal advisors and firms

4.5 Whistleblower Protections

Under the **Dodd-Frank Act**, whistleblowers are protected from retaliation and may be eligible for **monetary awards** if their report leads to enforcement action.

SECTION 5: REAL-WORLD ETHICAL SCENARIOS

SCENARIO 1: THE UNSOLICITED TRADE

A client asks you to buy a high-risk penny stock. You know it's a poor fit.

Do you:
✓ Decline and explain why?
✓ Execute it and cover yourself with the "unsolicited" label?

Correct Approach: Execute only if it's truly unsolicited, and **document it clearly** in the order ticket. Note your concerns to your supervisor.

SCENARIO 2: SWITCHING MUTUAL FUNDS FOR COMMISSION

You recommend a switch between two mutual funds that are almost identical—but from different families.

Do you:
✓ Highlight the switch benefits clearly?
✓ Consider alternative justifications?

Correct Approach: Only recommend if there's a **real benefit** (e.g., better performance, fees, or fit). Switching just for commission = **violation**.

SCENARIO 3: RECOMMENDING VARIABLE ANNUITIES TO SENIORS

A 70-year-old client with no investment experience is offered a complex VA.

Do you:

- Fully disclose all fees and riders?
- Consider suitability based on their age and liquidity needs?

Correct Approach: Thoroughly explain all features and risks. If unsure, consult a supervisor or recommend a more appropriate product.

SCENARIO 4: PROMOTING A PROPRIETARY FUND

Your firm pushes you to sell in-house products for higher commissions.

Do you:

- Tell the client it's the best option without comparison?
- Disclose other options?

Correct Approach: Disclose the conflict. Offer multiple suitable options when available.

Conclusion: Ethics Is Not a Choice — It's the Profession

As a securities professional, your actions must reflect not only technical competence but also:

- Moral clarity
- Transparency
- Unwavering client loyalty

Your ethical judgment will be tested both on the exam and in the field. Remember:

- Always disclose conflicts of interest
- Only recommend what is best for the client
- Never mislead or withhold material facts

CHAPTER 10
COMMUNICATION WITH CLIENTS AND PROSPECTS

In the financial services industry, what you say—and how you say it—can make the difference between client trust and regulatory trouble. Whether you're sending an email, running a seminar, posting a video online, or responding to a complaint, every form of communication is subject to strict rules.

This chapter covers:

✓ The different types of client communications
✓ Advertising and social media compliance
✓ Responding to complaints
✓ Supervisory responsibilities over reps' communications

The Series 63 exam will test your ability to recognize compliant and non-compliant statements, disclosures, and documentation practices.

SECTION 1: TYPES OF CLIENT COMMUNICATION

1.1 Overview: What Constitutes a Communication?

A communication includes any message intended for a client or prospect, regardless of form. This includes:

✓ Emails, letters, and newsletters
✓ Phone calls and voicemails
✓ Text messages and social media posts
✓ In-person seminars and investor events
✓ Advertisements, websites, and brochures

Every communication is subject to review under state securities laws and firm policies.

1.2 Categories of Communication (FINRA Rule 2210 Reference)

Even though Series 63 is a state exam, it frequently references FINRA's communication framework. Communications are broken into:

Type	Definition
Correspondence	≤25 retail clients within any 30-day period
Retail Communication	>25 retail clients within a 30-day period (includes social media and ads)
Institutional Communication	Directed only to institutional clients (banks, BDs, IAs)

Retail communication has the highest regulatory scrutiny.

1.3 Principal Approval Requirements

Type of Communication	Principal Pre-Approval Required?
Correspondence	No, but subject to supervision
Retail Communication	Yes, before first use
Institutional Communication	No, but must be reviewed regularly

1.4 Static vs. Interactive Social Media

Social media is a **compliance hot zone**. There's a difference between:

✓ Static content (e.g., LinkedIn profile, YouTube video) → Requires pre-approval
✓ Interactive content (e.g., Facebook comments, Twitter replies) → Requires supervision, not pre-approval

Your firm must:
✓ Archive all business-related posts
✓ Prohibit "guaranteed return" claims or misleading statements
✓ Clearly disclose your firm affiliation and registration status

SECTION 2: ADVERTISING AND SALES LITERATURE REGULATIONS

2.1 Defining Advertising and Sales Literature

Advertising includes:
✓ TV, radio, online video or audio
✓ Paid search engine results or social ads

Sales literature includes:
✓ Brochures, pitch decks
✓ Fact sheets, fund performance charts
✓ Seminar handouts

Both must:
✓ Be fair and balanced
✓ Avoid exaggerated claims
✓ Include appropriate disclosures and disclaimers

2.2 Prohibited Practices in Advertising

You **may not**:
✓ Guarantee profits or claim returns are "safe"
✓ Imply registration equals endorsement or skill

✓ Use testimonials that promise results or hide risks
✓ Cite outdated performance data without context

Examples:

"This fund is your best retirement option—guaranteed."

"This fund has outperformed its benchmark for 3 of the last 5 years. Past performance is not a guarantee of future results."

2.3 Required Disclosures

All advertisements and sales materials must include:

✓ The name of the broker-dealer or investment adviser
✓ Principal address and contact info
✓ Clear risk disclosures
✓ A statement like: "Securities offered through [BD name], Member FINRA/SIPC"

For investment company products:

✓ Average annual total returns over 1-, 5-, and 10-year periods must be presented
✓ Disclose the maximum sales load or fees
✓ Use current performance data

2.4 Use of Rankings and Awards

If your firm uses third-party rankings:

✓ Clearly state the source of the ranking
✓ Explain the criteria used
✓ Note if the firm paid to be included

Failure to disclose this can be deemed deceptive.

2.5 Seminars and Public Appearances

When hosting or speaking at public events:

✓ Submit scripts and handouts for review
✓ Avoid "selling" proprietary products unless clearly disclosed
✓ Never imply investment outcomes

You must also:
✓ Disclose registration jurisdiction
✓ Log attendee details for compliance follow-up

SECTION 3: ELECTRONIC AND WRITTEN COMMUNICATION POLICIES

3.1 Email and Text Messaging Rules

Firms must:

✓ Archive all business-related emails and texts
✓ Review random samples periodically
✓ Prohibit use of unauthorized messaging platforms (e.g., WhatsApp)

Reps must never:
✓ Discuss client investments over personal email
✓ Delete or alter any communication records
✓ Send account numbers or sensitive data unencrypted

3.2 Business Cards, Email Signatures, and Disclaimers

All written business identifiers must include:

✓ Your full legal name
✓ Title and registration (e.g., Registered Representative)
✓ Your firm's name and contact details
✓ State-specific disclosures, where applicable

Example email footer:
"John Smith, Registered Representative | ABC Securities, Member FINRA/SIPC"

3.3 Client Disclosures and Delivery Requirements

Certain documents must be:
✓ Delivered before or at the time of the transaction
✓ Filed with the Administrator, depending on content

Required delivery includes:
✓ Prospectus (for mutual funds and VAs)
✓ Privacy notices (under Regulation S-P)
✓ Form CRS (for broker-dealer/investment adviser firms)

SECTION 4: HANDLING CLIENT COMPLAINTS AND INQUIRIES

4.1 What Constitutes a Complaint?

A complaint is:
Any **written communication** alleging a grievance or expressing dissatisfaction with a rep's conduct, investment strategy, or firm behavior.

Oral complaints must be logged **if material**, but only written ones are subject to **mandatory regulatory tracking**.

4.2 Complaint Handling Process

Step	Action
Receive the complaint	Document it immediately and date-stamp
Notify a supervisor	Do not try to resolve it alone
Acknowledge to the client	Send a written receipt or response promptly

Investigate internally	Review documentation, emails, call logs
Respond and remediate	If necessary, offer a remedy or explain findings

All actions must be documented in the firm's complaint log, which is reviewed during regulatory audits.

4.3 Escalation Protocols

Escalate to:
✓ Legal/compliance if there are threats of legal action
✓ FINRA or the state administrator if requested by regulators
✓ Principal for any concerns involving suitability or unauthorized trades

You must never:
✓ Admit fault without authorization
✓ Offer to "make it right" out of your own pocket
✓ Delay reporting or alter records after a complaint is made

4.4 Complaint Records and Retention

Under FINRA Rule 4513 and state rules:

✓ Complaint records must be kept for 4 years
✓ They must be accessible for inspection by regulators
✓ Annual reviews of complaint logs are required by firm compliance departments

SECTION 5: ETHICAL AND COMPLIANT COMMUNICATION SCENARIOS

SCENARIO 1: SOCIAL MEDIA POST ABOUT INVESTMENT RETURNS

You post:
"The ABC Fund returned 12% last year—invest today and retire rich!"

Correct Practice:
Include a disclaimer, current prospectus link, time frame of performance, and note: "Past performance is not indicative of future results."

SCENARIO 2: RESPONDING TO A TEXT MESSAGE TRADE REQUEST

Client texts:
"Buy $10k of the Growth Fund for me."

Correct Practice:
Don't respond or execute the order via text. Call the client or redirect the request through a firm-approved channel and document the order properly.

SCENARIO 3: A COMPLAINING CLIENT THREATENS A LAWSUIT

Client writes a complaint letter claiming unsuitable advice and financial loss.

Correct Practice:
Do not reply directly. Forward to compliance immediately. The firm will draft a formal response, initiate investigation, and retain legal counsel if necessary.

Scenario 4: Brochure Mentions "Risk-Free" Product
Your new brochure calls a variable annuity "a safe, risk-free investment."

Correct Practice:
Remove or revise the language. All products carry some level of risk, especially variable annuities. Misleading terms can result in sanctions.

Conclusion: Compliance Is Communication

Your communications—spoken, written, or posted—must reflect the same ethics and professionalism you bring to every trade and every client meeting. Never forget:

✓ Clear communication protects your client
✓ Proper disclosures protect you
✓ Prompt complaint handling protects your firm

As you prepare for the Series 63 exam and your ongoing career, remember that in every message you send, you're also sending a signal about your integrity.

CHAPTER 11
REMEDIES AND ADMINISTRATIVE PROVISIONS

No matter how tightly securities laws are crafted, violations still occur—some by mistake, others willfully. That's why every state securities law, including the Uniform Securities Act (USA), includes a structured framework for investigation, enforcement, and remedies.

This chapter walks you through:

✓ The investigative powers granted to administrators
✓ Civil and criminal penalties for various infractions
✓ Legal remedies available to harmed investors
✓ Your rights and responsibilities as a securities professional if you're ever the subject of regulatory action

Understanding these procedures is not just about passing the **Series 63**—it's about recognizing how justice is enforced and how client trust is restored.

SECTION 1: INVESTIGATIONS AND ENFORCEMENT ACTIONS

1.1 Powers of the State Securities Administrator

Under the USA, each state designates a Securities Administrator empowered to:

✓ Investigate potential violations
✓ Enforce the Act through legal and administrative means
✓ Take action to prevent fraud and protect the investing public

1.2 Investigation Authority
Administrators may:

✓ Initiate formal or informal investigations
✓ Conduct on-site inspections of firms and records
✓ Investigate both in-state and out-of-state activity
✓ Act with or without prior notice or cause

They are not required to wait for a client complaint. Suspicion or proactive audits can justify an investigation.

1.3 Subpoenas and Testimony
Administrators may issue:

✓ Subpoenas for documents, transaction records, and communications
✓ Subpoenas duces tecum (require specific documents)
✓ Orders compelling testimony under oath

Failing to comply can result in:
✓ Contempt of court
✓ Temporary injunctions or restraining orders
✓ Civil or criminal prosecution

Investigative powers under the USA extend across **state lines**, making cooperation mandatory even if the rep or firm is located elsewhere.

1.4 Enforcement Tools Available to the Administrator

Tool	Used To
Cease and Desist Order	Stop suspicious activity immediately—can be issued without a hearing
Injunction (via courts)	Obtain a court order to legally prohibit ongoing or future violations
Restitution	Order return of funds to harmed investors
Administrative Fines	Penalize violations without criminal prosecution
License Suspension/ Revocation	Deny or terminate registration of agents or firms

A "cease and desist" order is administrative. An "injunction" is a legal order issued through the courts.

SECTION 2: CIVIL AND CRIMINAL PENALTIES

2.1 Civil Penalties: When the Law Is Broken but Not Willfully

Civil liability arises when an agent or firm violates securities laws through negligence, misrepresentation, or improper registration—even if they didn't intend harm.

Examples of Civil Violations:

✓ Selling unregistered, non-exempt securities
✓ Failing to disclose material information
✓ Providing unsuitable recommendations
✓ Acting as an unregistered agent
✓ Omitting facts that would have altered the investor's decision

2.2 Civil Liability Provisions (USA §410)

Investors harmed by a civil violation can:

✓ Sue the violating party
✓ Request rescission (undoing the trade)
✓ Demand interest, court costs, and reasonable attorney's fees

Rescission is the legal equivalent of hitting "undo" on a securities transaction.

2.3 Statute of Limitations

Civil actions must be filed within the earlier of:

✓ 3 years of the violation or
✓ 2 years from the date the investor discovered (or should have discovered) the violation

This encourages prompt claims while protecting firms from indefinite exposure.

2.4 Who Can Be Held Liable?

Multiple parties can face civil liability:

✓ Broker-dealers and investment advisers
✓ Agents and IARs
✓ Supervisory principals
✓ Anyone who aided or abetted the violation

2.5 Criminal Penalties: For Willful Violations

Criminal liability occurs when a person:

✓ Willfully violates any provision of the USA
✓ Knowingly commits fraud or deception
✓ Acts with intent to deceive or defraud

This includes:
✓ Insider trading
✓ Forgery or falsified documents
✓ Knowingly misleading advertising
✓ Fraudulent Ponzi schemes or sales practices

2.6 Criminal Penalty Limits

Under the USA, criminal violations may result in:

✓ Fines up to $5,000 per offense
✓ Imprisonment for up to 3 years
✓ Both fine and imprisonment

Criminal actions are usually prosecuted by the state attorney general—not the administrator.

2.7 Key Differences between Civil and Criminal Violations

Aspect	Civil	Criminal
Intent Required	No (negligence or error may suffice)	Yes (willful and knowing actions)
Initiated By	Investor (private lawsuit) or Administrator	Prosecutor or Attorney General
Possible Penalties	Fines, restitution, rescission	Fines, prison, loss of license
Standard of Proof	Preponderance of evidence	Beyond a reasonable doubt

SECTION 3: RIGHTS OF RESCISSION AND RESTITUTION

3.1 What Is Rescission?

Rescission is the legal right of an investor to reverse a securities transaction and be made financially whole.

It applies when:
✓ The security was sold unlawfully
✓ The investor was misled
✓ The agent or firm violated registration rules or fiduciary obligations

Rescission is the investor's remedy—but if the investor refuses rescission, they may waive their right to sue.

3.2 Rescission Process
If a firm or agent discovers a violation:

1. Offer rescission to the affected investor
2. Include full repayment plus interest, minus any income already received (e.g., dividends)
3. Give the investor 30 days to accept or reject

If accepted:
✓ No further legal action may be taken
✓ The matter is settled civilly

If rejected or ignored:
✓ The investor may pursue a civil lawsuit

3.3 Restitution and Disgorgement
Restitution is broader than rescission—it may involve:
✓ Paying back money lost due to misconduct

✓ Compensating for improper fees or commissions
✓ Returning gains derived from unethical or illegal conduct

In severe cases, courts may order:
Disgorgement: Forcing the violator to surrender all ill-gotten profits

3.4 When Rescission Is Not Enough

If an investor:
✓ Suffers emotional damages
✓ Faces extended financial loss
✓ Incurs legal fees beyond rescission

They may pursue additional damages under state tort or securities fraud laws—though this is rare and difficult to prove.

SECTION 4: ADMINISTRATIVE SANCTIONS AND DUE PROCESS

4.1 Denial, Suspension, and Revocation of Registration

Administrators may take disciplinary action against:

✓ Agents
✓ Broker-dealers
✓ Investment advisers
✓ Issuers

Possible actions:
✓ Deny an initial application
✓ Suspend existing registration
✓ Revoke registration permanently
✓ Bar individuals from future licensure

4.2 Grounds for Administrative Action

Grounds for Sanction	Examples
False statements on application	Omitting past bankruptcies, felonies, or regulatory actions
Conviction of felony or securities-related misdemeanor	Within the past **10 years**

Insolvency or financial failure	Firm unable to meet capital requirements
Willful violation of securities laws	Fraud, misrepresentation, selling unregistered securities
Failure to supervise	A supervisor fails to monitor a subordinate's illegal conduct
Disqualification by another regulator	Barred or suspended by FINRA, SEC, or another state administrator

4.3 Due Process Protections

Before taking disciplinary action, administrators must provide:
✓ Notice of the proceeding
✓ Opportunity for a hearing
✓ Written findings of fact and law

Hearings typically occur **within** 15–30 days of the notice and allow for:
✓ Representation by counsel
✓ Presentation of evidence and witnesses
✓ A full defense by the accused party

No registration can be revoked retroactively—only from the date of the order forward.

4.4 Summary Actions and Emergency Powers

In urgent cases, the administrator may issue a:

✓ Summary order (e.g., cease and desist) without a prior hearing
✓ The respondent may later request a hearing to contest it
✓ Such orders remain in effect until overturned or expired

SECTION 5: KEY TAKEAWAYS AND CASE STUDY EXAMPLES

5.1 Summary of Investor Remedies

Remedy Type	Who Can Use It	When Applied
Rescission	Investors	After illegal/unethical transaction
Civil Lawsuit	Investors/Regulators	For compensation and court action
Criminal Prosecution	Attorney General	For intentional, willful fraud
Administrative Orders	State Administrator	For suspension, fines, and injunctions

5.2 Case Study: Unauthorized Trading

Scenario:
An agent executes two trades in a client's account without written or oral authorization.

Remedy:
✓ The administrator suspends the agent's license.
✓ The client receives a rescission offer and accepts.
✓ Civil liability is avoided, but the rep's record is permanently affected.

5.3 Case Study: Selling Unregistered Securities

Scenario:
A rep sells a new digital asset fund to 12 clients in their state. The fund was not registered and did not qualify for exemption.

Outcome:
✓ Administrator issues cease-and-desist
✓ Clients sue for rescission
✓ Firm pays restitution and fines
✓ Rep is barred from practice for 5 years

CONCLUSION: RESPONSIBILITY DOESN'T END WITH THE SALE

Understanding remedies and enforcement is about more than just knowing penalties. It's about accountability. Securities professionals:

✓ Must act carefully and ethically
✓ Should self-report violations or errors
✓ Need to understand how restitution works
✓ Must never assume ignorance is a shield

Your knowledge of this chapter won't just help you pass the Series 63 exam—it will help you stay compliant, protect your firm, and protect your clients in the real world.

CHAPTER 12
PRACTICE QUESTIONS FOR SERIES 6

100 MULTIPLE-CHOICE QUESTIONS WITH DETAILED EXPLANATIONS

Question 1
Which of the following securities can be sold under the Series 6 license?

A. Corporate bonds
B. Municipal bonds
C. Variable annuities
D. Options contracts

Correct Answer: C. Variable annuities

Explanation:
Series 6 licensees can sell mutual funds, variable annuities, unit investment trusts (UITs), and 529 plans. They cannot sell individual stocks, bonds, or options. Variable annuities are packaged investment products and fall within Series 6 scope.

Question 2

A registered representative recommends a mutual fund with a high front-end load but fails to disclose a similar no-load alternative. What rule has likely been violated?

A. Regulation T
B. FINRA Rule 2210
C. Suitability
D. Fair Dealing and Disclosure

Correct Answer: D. Fair Dealing and Disclosure

Explanation:

Reps are required to act fairly and disclose material facts. Failing to mention a no-load alternative is misleading and may violate FINRA's principles of fair dealing and ethical practice.

Question 3

Which investment is **not** considered a redeemable security?

A. Mutual fund share
B. Variable annuity contract
C. Closed-end fund share
D. Unit investment trust (UIT) share

Correct Answer: C. Closed-end fund share

Explanation:

Closed-end funds trade on secondary markets like stocks and are not redeemable through the issuer. All others are redeemable directly with the sponsor or fund company.

Question 4

An investor in a variable annuity chooses the separate account. What is the primary reason for this?

A. Principal is guaranteed
B. Returns are fixed
C. Gains are tax-free
D. Potential for higher returns through market exposure

Correct Answer: D. Potential for higher returns through market exposure

Explanation:

Separate accounts in variable annuities allow investment in sub-accounts (like mutual funds) for market growth potential. They are not guaranteed and carry investment risk.

Question 5

What happens when a mutual fund pays a dividend?

A. NAV increases
B. NAV decreases
C. NAV stays the same
D. It depends on fund performance

Correct Answer: B. NAV decreases

Explanation:

When a fund distributes dividends, the net asset value (NAV) drops by the same amount per share because assets are reduced.

Question 6

A client wants both tax deferral and life insurance benefits. Which product is most suitable?

A. Term life insurance
B. Universal life insurance
C. Traditional IRA
D. Variable annuity

Correct Answer: B. Universal life insurance

Explanation:

Universal life combines life insurance with a cash value component that grows tax-deferred. While variable annuities offer tax deferral, they do not provide life insurance death benefits in the same way.

Question 7

Which of the following is **not** a characteristic of open-end investment companies?

A. Continuous issuance of new shares
B. Shares traded on an exchange
C. Priced at NAV
D. Must redeem shares at NAV

Correct Answer: B. Shares traded on an exchange

Explanation:

Only closed-end funds trade on exchanges. Open-end funds (mutual funds) are bought and redeemed directly with the fund company.

Question 8

Under FINRA rules, which of the following **must** be approved by a principal before use?

A. Internal email between reps
B. Social media "likes"
C. Retail communication
D. Institutional communication

Correct Answer: C. Retail communication

Explanation:
Retail communication (e.g., ads, websites, brochures aimed at >25 retail investors) must be pre-approved by a principal. Institutional communication does not require pre-approval unless reused with retail clients.

Question 9
What is the primary benefit of dollar-cost averaging?
A. Guarantees profits
B. Reduces taxes
C. Spreads investment risk over time
D. Maximizes dividends

Correct Answer: C. Spreads investment risk over time

Explanation:
Dollar-cost averaging involves investing equal amounts at regular intervals, reducing the impact of market volatility by buying more shares when prices are low and fewer when high.

Question 10
An investor has a low risk tolerance and needs regular income. Which fund is most suitable?

A. Aggressive growth fund
B. High-yield bond fund

C. Money market fund
D. Emerging markets fund

Correct Answer: C. Money market fund

Explanation:
Money market funds are low-risk, offer liquidity, and provide modest income. High-yield or emerging market funds are **too volatile** for conservative investors.

Question 11
How often must a mutual fund send semiannual reports to shareholders?

A. Annually
B. Every 6 months
C. Every 3 months
D. Monthly

Correct Answer: B. Every 6 months

Explanation:
Mutual funds are required by the SEC to send **semiannual reports** (every 6 months) to shareholders, including performance and financial data.

Question 12
Which of the following is an example of breakpoint sales abuse?

A. Offering a client a discount at $100,000
B. Explaining rights of accumulation
C. Failing to inform a client they are $5,000 from a breakpoint
D. Suggesting an A-share mutual fund

Correct Answer: C. Failing to inform a client they are $5,000 from a breakpoint

Explanation:
This denies the investor a sales charge discount and violates FINRA and SEC rules on fair dealing. Reps must inform clients when they're near breakpoints.

Question 13
Which of the following is not a function of a transfer agent?

A. Canceling old shares
B. Recording share ownership
C. Safekeeping securities
D. Issuing new shares

Correct Answer: C. Safekeeping securities

Explanation:
Custodians handle safekeeping. Transfer agents handle recordkeeping, issuance, and shareholder services.

Question 14
What is the max contribution limit for a Coverdell ESA in 2025?

A. $500
B. $1,000
C. $2,000
D. Unlimited

Correct Answer: C. $2,000

Explanation:
As of current rules, the maximum annual contribution to a Coverdell ESA is $2,000 per beneficiary.

Question 15

What does a variable annuity accumulation unit represent?

A. The payout value
B. Ownership in the general account
C. Participation in subaccounts
D. The death benefit

Correct Answer: C. Participation in subaccounts

Explanation:

During the accumulation phase, clients buy accumulation units that reflect ownership in investment subaccounts. These convert to annuity units in retirement.

Question 16

What is the NAV per share if a mutual fund has $50 million in assets and 5 million shares outstanding?

A. $10
B. $50
C. $5
D. $25

Correct Answer: A. $10

Explanation:

NAV = Total Assets ÷ Shares Outstanding = $50 million ÷ 5 million = $10 per share

Question 17
When must a registered rep complete regulatory element continuing education?

A. Only at renewal
B. Every 5 years
C. Annually
D. By their second registration anniversary and every 3 years after

Correct Answer: D. By their second registration anniversary and every 3 years after

Explanation:
FINRA requires registered reps to complete **regulatory element CE** on a 3-year cycle starting **2 years after registration**.

Question 18
A registered rep recommends frequent switching between mutual funds. This could be seen as:

A. Breakpoint fraud
B. Market timing
C. Churning
D. Trading-on-the-margin

Correct Answer: C. Churning

Explanation:
Churning is excessive trading in a client's account to generate commissions. It violates suitability and fair practice rules.

Question 19
A principal must approve which of the following before execution?

A. Internal correspondence
B. Market orders
C. New account applications
D. Daily trade blotters

Correct Answer: C. New account applications

Explanation:

All new accounts must be approved by a principal before any trading. This ensures suitability and regulatory compliance.

Question 20
The prospectus for a mutual fund must be provided to an investor:

A. Before any discussion about the fund
B. Within 3 days after the purchase
C. At or before the confirmation of the sale
D. Immediately upon account opening

Correct Answer: C. At or before the confirmation of the sale

Question 21
Which of the following would most likely be considered a redeemable security?

A. Common stock
B. Preferred stock
C. Mutual fund share
D. Exchange-traded fund (ETF)

Correct Answer: C. Mutual fund share

Explanation:
Mutual funds are redeemable directly with the issuer. Stocks and ETFs are traded on secondary markets and are not redeemable in the same manner.

Question 22
What is the primary regulatory concern when a rep makes exaggerated performance claims?

A. Market manipulation
B. Misrepresentation
C. Insider trading
D. Churning

Correct Answer: B. Misrepresentation

Explanation:
Overstating returns or guarantees violates FINRA's rules against false or misleading statements — a form of misrepresentation.

Question 23
Under the Investment Company Act of 1940, which of the following is required?

A. Redemption within 14 days
B. Minimum capital of $50 million
C. Shareholder voting for investment adviser changes
D. Daily NAV calculation

Correct Answer: C. Shareholder voting for investment adviser changes

Explanation:
A mutual fund must obtain shareholder approval to change its investment adviser. NAV is typically calculated daily, but it's not a statutory mandate.

Question 24
Which client is most suitable for a variable annuity?

A. 22-year-old college student
B. 70-year-old seeking short-term income
C. 50-year-old with a long-term retirement horizon
D. 40-year-old needing emergency funds

Correct Answer: C. 50-year-old with a long-term retirement horizon

Explanation:
Variable annuities are best for long-term retirement-focused investors. Early withdrawals are penalized, and they are not liquid for emergencies.

Question 25
Which of the following is **not** a regulated communication under FINRA Rule 2210?

A. Billboard ad for a mutual fund
B. Blog post about retirement planning
C. Email between two employees
D. A scripted client seminar

Correct Answer: C. Email between two employees

Explanation:
Internal emails between employees are not considered retail or public communication under FINRA 2210.

Question 26
What does the surrender charge in a variable annuity represent?

A. Tax penalty
B. Sales commission
C. Early withdrawal fee imposed by the IRS
D. Fee charged by the insurance company for early withdrawals

Correct Answer: D. Fee charged by the insurance company for early withdrawals

Explanation:

Surrender charges are fees imposed by the annuity issuer, not the IRS, when the contract is liquidated early (usually within 5–7 years).

Question 27
Which investment offers professional management, diversification, and redeemability?

A. Hedge fund
B. ETF
C. Mutual fund
D. Treasury bond

Correct Answer: C. Mutual fund

Explanation:
Mutual funds offer diversification, active management, and are redeemable at NAV. ETFs are diversified but traded like stocks, not redeemed.

Question 28

Who is responsible for issuing mutual fund shares?

A. Underwriter
B. Custodian
C. Transfer agent
D. Investment adviser

Correct Answer: C. Transfer agent

Explanation:

The transfer agent issues and redeems shares, maintains ownership records, and sends investor documents. The underwriter markets the fund, but does not issue shares.

Question 29

An investor buys mutual fund shares and is told she'll receive a prospectus. When must this be delivered?

A. Within 5 days of opening the account
B. At or before the purchase confirmation
C. After the first quarterly statement
D. Only if she requests it

Correct Answer: B. At or before the purchase confirmation

Explanation:

SEC rules require delivery of the prospectus at or before the confirmation of sale — even in electronic format.

Question 30

Which of the following has the lowest risk?

A. Sector mutual fund
B. Balanced fund
C. Money market fund
D. Emerging markets fund

Correct Answer: C. Money market fund

Explanation:

Money market funds invest in short-term, high-quality debt and are considered low-risk and low-return. Sector and emerging market funds carry much more volatility.

Question 31

The suitability rule requires that recommendations:

A. Guarantee no losses
B. Are appropriate for the customer's goals and risk tolerance
C. Always be written and signed
D. Include at least three product options

Correct Answer: B. Are appropriate for the customer's goals and risk tolerance

Explanation:

The core of FINRA's suitability rule is making recommendations in the best interest of the client's financial profile.

Question 32
What is the primary role of the investment adviser in a mutual fund?

A. Pricing the shares
B. Holding the fund's cash
C. Managing the fund's portfolio
D. Selling shares to the public

Correct Answer: C. Managing the fund's portfolio

Explanation:
The investment adviser makes the day-to-day investment decisions for the mutual fund's portfolio.

Question 33
Which type of mutual fund charges **a sales fee upon purchase?**

A. Class A shares
B. Class B shares
C. No-load shares
D. Class C shares

Correct Answer: A. Class A shares

Explanation:
Class A shares charge a front-end load (upfront sales charge). Class B typically ha

Question 34
An investor buys mutual fund shares with dividends reinvested. What tax consequences occur?

A. No tax due until shares are sold
B. Dividends are taxed annually

C. Dividends are taxed only at sale
D. Only capital gains are taxed annually

Correct Answer: B. Dividends are taxed annually

Explanation:
Even if reinvested, dividends and capital gains distributions are taxable in the year received.

Question 35
A mutual fund's expense ratio measures:

A. Operating costs as a percentage of total assets
B. Commissions paid to brokers
C. Shareholder profits
D. Load charges only

Correct Answer: A. Operating costs as a percentage of total assets

Explanation:

The expense ratio includes management fees, administrative costs, and 12b-1 fees, expressed as a percentage of average net assets.

Question 36
Which account type is most appropriate for a 529 Plan?

A. Individual brokerage account
B. Custodial account under UTMA
C. Educational savings account
D. Tax-deferred investment account

Correct Answer: C. Educational savings account

Explanation:
529 plans are specialized education savings accounts, offering tax advantages for qualified education expenses.

Question 37
Which of the following cannot be sold by a Series 6 representative?

A. Unit Investment Trust (UIT)
B. Variable life insurance
C. Index mutual fund
D. Treasury bond

Correct Answer: D. Treasury bond

Explanation:
Series 6 reps cannot sell individual securities, including government or corporate bonds. The other options are packaged products allowed under Series 6.

Question 38
What must be included in a mutual fund prospectus?

A. Performance over 1 year only
B. Analyst ratings
C. Investment objectives and risks
D. Personalized advice

Correct Answer: C. Investment objectives and risks

Explanation:
The prospectus is a disclosure document and must include the fund's objectives, fees, risks, and past performance data.

Question 39
What does the 12b-1 fee cover?

A. Commissions to fund managers
B. Custody and legal fees
C. Marketing and distribution expenses
D. Portfolio trading expenses

Correct Answer: C. Marketing and distribution expenses

Explanation:
12b-1 fees are annual charges taken from fund assets to pay for marketing, advertising, and sales commissions.

Question 40
Who supervises the day-to-day operations of a broker-dealer branch office?

A. Compliance officer

B. Series 6 representative
C. Registered principal
D. Financial and Operations Principal (FINOP)

Correct Answer: C. Registered principal

Explanation:
Branch office operations must be supervised by a registered principal, who reviews and approves communications, transactions, and customer interactions.

Question 41
Which of the following best describes a unit investment trust (UIT)?

A. A fund that reinvests all income
B. A managed investment portfolio
C. A fixed portfolio that terminates on a set date
D. An actively traded mutual fund

Correct Answer: C. A fixed portfolio that terminates on a set date

Explanation:
UITs are unmanaged investment companies that hold a fixed portfolio of securities and have a defined termination date. They don't have active managers.

Question 42
What is the maximum sales charge allowed on mutual funds under FINRA rules?

A. 4%
B. 5%
C. 8.5%
D. 10%

Correct Answer: C. 8.5%

Explanation:
According to FINRA and the Investment Company Act of 1940, mutual funds may charge a maximum sales load of 8.5% of the POP, provided they offer breakpoints and reinvestment privileges.

Question 43
A registered representative may describe a no-load fund as such only if:

A. The 12b-1 fee is less than 0.25%
B. It is offered by a bank

C. It invests only in government securities
D. The client does not pay a commission

Correct Answer: A. The 12b-1 fee is less than 0.25%

Explanation:
To be labeled no-load, a fund must have no front- or back-end sales charges and 12b-1 fees no greater than 0.25% annually.

Question 44
Which of the following must a representative do before opening a new account?

A. Determine the customer's occupation only
B. Obtain the client's written investment policy
C. Review customer suitability and financial goals
D. File a form with the SEC

Correct Answer: C. Review customer suitability and financial goals

Explanation:
Before recommending or opening an account, reps must collect data such as financial goals, income, risk tolerance, and investment experience to establish suitability.

Question 45
What type of fund is designed to match the performance of a particular index?

A. Sector fund
B. Index fund
C. Balanced fund
D. Fund of funds

Correct Answer: B. Index fund

Explanation:
An index fund passively replicates the performance of a specific benchmark like the S&P 500. These funds typically have lower expenses due to minimal trading.

Question 46
An investor in a mutual fund has the right to accumulate toward breakpoints by:

A. Purchasing only B shares
B. Having a good credit score
C. Using rights of accumulation
D. Making deposits into a checking account

Correct Answer: C. Using rights of accumulation

Explanation:
Rights of accumulation allow investors to use the total value of their existing holdings to qualify for a reduced sales charge on new purchases.

Question 47
Which of the following statements is **true** regarding Class B shares?

A. They charge a front-end load
B. They convert to Class A shares after a period
C. They are suitable for short-term investing
D. They offer breakpoints

Correct Answer: B. They convert to Class A shares after a period

Explanation:
Class B shares have back-end loads (CDSC) but convert to Class A shares (with lower expenses) after several years — usually 6–8 years.

Question 48
The custodian of a mutual fund is primarily responsible for:

A. Distributing dividends
B. Managing the portfolio
C. Holding the fund's assets in safekeeping
D. Pricing the fund

Correct Answer: C. Holding the fund's assets in safekeeping

Explanation:
The custodian bank holds the fund's cash and securities in safekeeping, separate from investment decisions made by the adviser.

Question 49
Which of the following can be marketed by a Series 6 representative?

A. Hedge funds
B. Individual stocks
C. Mutual funds
D. Corporate bonds

Correct Answer: C. Mutual funds

Explanation:
Series 6 reps are limited to packaged securities: mutual funds, variable products, 529 plans, and UITs. They cannot sell individual securities.

Question 50
A variable annuity owner is in the payout phase. What are the payments based on?

A. Number of accumulation units
B. NAV

C. Annuity units
D. Surrender value

Correct Answer: C. Annuity units

Explanation:
Once in the payout phase, the investor receives payments based on annuity units, which are calculated based on age, assumed interest rate (AIR), and payout option.

Question 51
Which entity is primarily responsible for setting the investment objective of a mutual fund?

A. The investment adviser
B. The custodian
C. The board of directors
D. The SEC

Correct Answer: C. The board of directors

Explanation:
The board of directors, representing shareholders, establishes the fund's investment objective and oversees management.

Question 52
What document is used to register new mutual fund shares with the SEC?

A. Form U4
B. Form BD
C. Registration statement
D. Subscription agreement

Correct Answer: C. Registration statement

Explanation:
Mutual fund issuers file a registration statement with the SEC, which includes information about the fund, objectives, fees, and risks.

Question 53
What kind of risk is least likely to affect a money market fund?

A. Inflation risk
B. Interest rate risk
C. Market risk
D. Liquidity risk

Correct Answer: D. Liquidity risk

Explanation:
Money market funds are highly liquid, making liquidity risk very low. However, they are susceptible to inflation risk and interest rate risk over time.

Question 54
What is the initial sales charge applied to a $10,000 purchase of Class A mutual fund shares with a 5% load?

A. $500
B. $476.19
C. $525.25
D. $450

Correct Answer: B. $476.19

Explanation:
Sales load = POP – NAV
So, if POP is 100%, NAV = 95%, meaning:
$10,000 × (5% / 105%) = $476.19

Question 55
Which of the following is **not** an objective of the FINRA suitability rule?

A. Understand the client's investment objectives
B. Guarantee positive returns
C. Evaluate risk tolerance
D. Assess financial condition

Correct Answer: B. Guarantee positive returns

Explanation:
Suitability ensures recommendations match client needs — but there's no guarantee of profits or positive returns.

Question 56
A customer wants tax deferral and is willing to invest long term. Which is most suitable?

A. Variable annuity
B. Treasury bond
C. REIT
D. Balanced mutual fund

Correct Answer: A. Variable annuity

Explanation:
Variable annuities offer tax-deferred growth, are appropriate for long-term investors, and allow for investment in subaccounts.

Question 57
A 12b-1 fee is typically expressed as:

A. A front-end load
B. A flat annual dollar amount
C. A percentage of net assets
D. A per-share fee

Correct Answer: C. A percentage of net assets

Explanation:
12b-1 fees are typically calculated as a percentage of average daily net assets, deducted annually for marketing and distribution.

Question 58
Who is responsible for reviewing and approving communications with the public?

A. FINRA examiner
B. Investment adviser
C. Registered principal
D. Registered rep

Correct Answer: C. Registered principal

Explanation:
FINRA requires a registered principal to review and approve all retail communications before use.

Question 59
Which investment offers the highest level of liquidity?

A. Variable annuity
B. Real estate investment trust (REIT)

C. Money market mutual fund
D. Closed-end fund

Correct Answer: C. Money market mutual fund

Explanation:
Money market funds are highly liquid and allow same-day redemption at NAV. Other investments are less liquid or subject to restrictions.

Question 60
When must a customer receive a statement of additional information (SAI)?

A. Automatically within 5 days
B. At account opening
C. Only upon request
D. At or before trade confirmation

Correct Answer: C. Only upon request

Explanation:
The SAI is not required to be automatically delivered with the prospectus but must be provided promptly upon request.

Question 61
An investor wants to avoid probate upon death. Which account registration method achieves this?

A. Individual account
B. UTMA account
C. Joint tenants with right of survivorship (JTWROS)
D. Joint tenants in common (JTIC)

Correct Answer: C. Joint tenants with right of survivorship (JTWROS)

Explanation:
JTWROS accounts automatically transfer ownership to the surviving tenant, bypassing probate. JTIC accounts do not provide this benefit.

Question 62
Which of the following can a Series 6 rep recommend?

A. Municipal bond fund
B. General obligation bonds
C. Callable preferred stock
D. Stock options

Correct Answer: A. Municipal bond fund

Explanation:
Series 6 representatives can recommend packaged products, like mutual funds. They cannot recommend individual securities, such as bonds or options.

Question 63
Which mutual fund share class typically has the lowest annual operating expenses?

A. Class A
B. Class B
C. Class C
D. No-load shares

Correct Answer: A. Class A

Explanation:
Class A shares usually carry a front-end load but have lower annual expenses compared to Class B or C shares, making them cost-effective for long-term investors.

Question 64
Which mutual fund feature minimizes tax liability for the investor?

A. Dividend reinvestment
B. Capital gains distribution
C. Tax-efficient fund management
D. High turnover rate

Correct Answer: C. Tax-efficient fund management

Explanation:
Funds that practice tax-efficient management (e.g., low turnover, tax-loss harvesting) reduce taxable events for investors.

Question 65
What is the main purpose of the Statement of Additional Information (SAI)?

A. Provide daily NAV
B. List fund executives' compensation and policies
C. Summarize tax benefits of the fund
D. Show fund performance compared to the index

Correct Answer: B. List fund executives' compensation and policies

Explanation:
The SAI contains detailed disclosures not found in the statutory prospectus, such as executive compensation, portfolio holdings, and legal structure.

Question 66

A customer requests an SAI. How soon must it be delivered?

A. Within 3 business days
B. At account opening
C. Within 7 calendar days
D. Promptly upon request

Correct Answer: D. Promptly upon request

Explanation:

While not automatically delivered, the SAI must be sent promptly upon customer request, typically within 3 business days.

Question 67

Which of the following must be retained by a broker-dealer for at least three years?

A. Customer complaints
B. Account statements
C. Advertising materials
D. New account forms

Correct Answer: C. Advertising materials

Explanation:

Under FINRA rules, communications with the public (ads, sales literature, social posts) must be kept for 3 years, with the first 2 years easily accessible.

Question 68

A client wants to avoid upfront sales charges and still invest in mutual funds. Which share class is appropriate?

A. Class A
B. Class B
C. Class C
D. No-load

Correct Answer: D. No-load

Explanation:
No-load funds charge no sales fees at purchase or redemption and minimal 12b-1 fees, making them ideal for cost-conscious investors.

Question 69
A registered representative cannot recommend a mutual fund unless they:

A. Have a Series 7 license
B. Hold the securities personally
C. Understand the product's risks and features
D. Provide a written investment policy

Correct Answer: C. Understand the product's risks and features

Explanation:
Reps must have reasonable grounds for suitability by understanding the structure, benefits, and risks of the product.

Question 70
Which fee is typically not included in a mutual fund's expense ratio?

A. Management fee
B. 12b-1 marketing fees
C. Custodial fees
D. Sales load

Correct Answer: D. Sales load

Explanation:
Sales loads (front-end or back-end) are transactional and not part of the expense ratio, which covers ongoing operational costs.

Question 71
What is the purpose of breakpoints in mutual funds?

A. Increase commission
B. Reduce NAV
C. Lower sales charges for larger investments
D. Trigger automatic redemption

Correct Answer: C. Lower sales charges for larger investments

Explanation:
Breakpoints are sales charge discounts given when investments reach certain thresholds, encouraging larger purchases.

Question 72
Which of the following is **not** regulated under the Investment Company Act of 1940?

A. UIT
B. Hedge fund
C. Mutual fund
D. Closed-end fund

Correct Answer: B. Hedge fund

Explanation:
Hedge funds are private placements, generally for accredited investors, and are not registered investment companies under the 1940 Act.

Question 73
A rep sells a fund with higher fees and no significant added benefit. This is likely:

A. Front-running
B. Switching
C. Churning
D. Breakpoint abuse

Correct Answer: B. Switching

Explanation:
Switching is when a rep moves clients between funds unnecessarily, often to generate commissions. It's a suitability violation unless it benefits the client.

Question 74
Which of the following mutual fund features is **guaranteed**?

A. NAV increase
B. Income payout
C. Liquidity
D. Capital appreciation

Correct Answer: C. Liquidity

Explanation:
Mutual funds are liquid investments, redeemable at NAV daily. Returns and income are not guaranteed.

Question 75
Who must review and approve new account applications?

A. Compliance department
B. Registered principal
C. FINRA examiner
D. Sales manager

Correct Answer: B. Registered principal

Explanation:
A principal must approve each new account before it can be activated or used for transactions.

Question 76
What is the main regulatory function of a prospectus?

A. Recommend the best product
B. Serve as an advertising tool
C. Disclose material facts to investors
D. Set the public offering price

Correct Answer: C. Disclose material facts to investors

Explanation:
The prospectus is a disclosure document required by the SEC to ensure investors are informed of the investment's risks, objectives, and fees.

Question 77
An investor is close to qualifying for a breakpoint. The rep should:

A. Ignore it
B. Suggest delaying the purchase
C. Encourage splitting purchases
D. Inform the investor of the opportunity

Correct Answer: D. Inform the investor of the opportunity

Explanation:
Failing to disclose available breakpoints is a serious violation. Reps must inform clients of all cost-saving options.

Question 78
Which document is used to change a variable annuity's beneficiary?

A. Insurance amendment form
B. Prospectus supplement
C. Change-of-beneficiary form
D. Letter of instruction

Correct Answer: C. Change-of-beneficiary form

Explanation:
To update beneficiaries, clients must file a change-of-beneficiary form with the insurance company.

Question 79
What is an advantage of investing in mutual funds over individual securities?

A. Guaranteed higher returns
B. No risk of principal loss
C. Access to leverage
D. Professional management and diversification

Correct Answer: D. Professional management and diversification

Explanation:
Mutual funds provide instant diversification and are managed by licensed professionals, reducing individual security selection risk.

Question 80
If an investor redeems mutual fund shares within 30 days of purchase, what might apply?

A. 12b-1 fee
B. Short-term redemption fee
C. Surrender charge
D. Breakpoint reinstatement

Correct Answer: B. Short-term redemption fee

Explanation:
Some funds charge a short-term redemption fee to discourage rapid turnover. This is separate from any sales load.

Question 81
Which of the following distributions from a mutual fund is typically taxable in the year received?

A. Unrealized capital gain
B. Dividend reinvestment
C. Return of capital
D. Exchange into another fund within the same family

Correct Answer: B. Dividend reinvestment

Explanation:
Even if reinvested, dividends are taxable in the year received. Unrealized gains are not taxed, and return of capital reduces cost basis.

Question 82
A Letter of Intent (LOI) allows an investor to:
A. Switch between fund families

B. Lock in current NAV for 90 days
C. Receive a breakpoint discount immediately
D. Redeem shares without penalty

Correct Answer: C. Receive a breakpoint discount immediately

Explanation:
An LOI states the investor's intent to invest a certain amount within 13 months, qualifying them for an immediate sales charge discount.

Question 83

Which of the following would best describe a Class C mutual fund share?

A. High upfront sales charge
B. High deferred sales charge after 5 years
C. No load but higher annual expenses
D. No deferred sales charge at all

Correct Answer: C. No load but higher annual expenses

Explanation:
Class C shares typically have no front-end load, a small deferred sales charge, and higher annual fees, making them less ideal for long-term investors.

Question 84
Which type of investment company has a fixed portfolio and no active management?

A. Mutual fund
B. Closed-end fund
C. Variable annuity

D. Unit investment trust (UIT)

Correct Answer: D. Unit investment trust (UIT)

Explanation:
UITs offer a fixed portfolio, no portfolio manager, and terminate on a set date, unlike mutual funds, which are actively managed.

Question 85
Which document lists all material information about a mutual fund?

A. Confirmation statement

B. Sales literature
C. Prospectus
D. Transfer form

Correct Answer: C. Prospectus

Explanation:
The prospectus is the main disclosure document that details objectives, fees, risks, performance, and management.

Question 86

An investor wants a fund with exposure to both stocks and bonds. What should you recommend?

A. Sector fund
B. Growth fund
C. Balanced fund
D. Money market fund

Correct Answer: C. Balanced fund

Explanation:
Balanced funds invest in both equity and fixed-income securities, offering a mix of growth and income potential.

Question 87
Which of the following is true about dollar-cost averaging?

A. It ensures a higher rate of return
B. It buys fewer shares when prices are low
C. It helps reduce average cost per share over time
D. It guarantees no loss

Correct Answer: C. It helps reduce average cost per share over time

Explanation:
Dollar-cost averaging spreads purchases over time, buying more shares when prices are low, potentially reducing average cost per share.

Question 88
Which party in a mutual fund is responsible for buying and selling securities in the portfolio?

A. Custodian
B. Board of Directors
C. Underwriter
D. Investment Adviser

Correct Answer: D. Investment Adviser

Explanation:
The investment adviser manages the portfolio on a daily basis, making decisions based on the fund's objective.

Question 89
What is a risk unique to variable annuities compared to fixed annuities?

A. Taxation on growth
B. Inflation risk
C. Market risk
D. Illiquidity

Correct Answer: C. Market risk

Explanation:
Variable annuities invest in subaccounts tied to the market, exposing the investor to market fluctuations, unlike fixed annuities.

Question 90
A customer receives a breakpoint discount and later redeems the shares. The rep must:

A. Pay back the difference
B. File a report with FINRA
C. Do nothing, since redemption is allowed
D. Re-calculate the sales charge

Correct Answer: C. Do nothing, since redemption is allowed

Explanation:
Breakpoints are based on amount invested, not how long the shares are held. Redemption does not invalidate the discount.

Question 91
What is the main difference between an open-end and closed-end fund?

A. Liquidity
B. Issuer type

C. Management style
D. Where the shares are traded

Correct Answer: D. Where the shares are traded

Explanation:
Closed-end funds trade on exchanges like stocks. Open-end funds (mutual funds) are bought and redeemed directly from the fund.

Question 92
If a fund's NAV is $18.25 and the POP is $19.25, what is the sales charge percentage?

A. 5.5%
B. 6.5%
C. 5.19%
D. 4.8%

Correct Answer: A. 5.5%

Explanation:
Sales charge = (POP - NAV) ÷ POP = (19.25 - 18.25) ÷ 19.25 = 0.052 or 5.5%

Question 93
A mutual fund's NAV is determined by:

A. Current market price of the shares
B. The board of directors
C. Total assets minus liabilities divided by shares outstanding
D. Demand and supply in the secondary market

Correct Answer: C. Total assets minus liabilities divided by shares outstanding

Explanation:
NAV = (Assets – Liabilities) / Shares Outstanding. It is calculated at the end of each trading day.

Question 94
Which fund typically avoids taxable distributions by replicating a benchmark?

A. Target-date fund
B. Balanced fund
C. Index fund
D. Sector fund

Correct Answer: C. Index fund

Explanation:
Index funds have low turnover, reducing taxable capital gains distributions, making them more tax-efficient.

Question 95
What is a switch letter used for?

A. Changing fund families
B. Explaining why a rep is moving a client from one fund to another
C. Disclosing fund expenses
D. Requesting a refund

Correct Answer: B. Explaining why a rep is moving a client from one fund to another

Explanation:
Switch letters document and justify fund switches, protecting the rep and firm from suitability violations.

Question 96
Which of the following does not affect a fund's NAV?

A. Sale of shares to investors
B. Dividend distributions
C. Change in portfolio value
D. Redemption of shares

Correct Answer: A. Sale of shares to investors

Explanation:
Issuing new shares does not affect NAV, since the fund receives cash in exchange. NAV fluctuates with the market value of holdings.

Question 97
An investor who wants to invest in mutual funds without incurring sales charges should choose:

A. Class A shares
B. Class B shares
C. No-load shares
D. Index funds only

Correct Answer: C. No-load shares

Explanation:
No-load funds do not charge a sales commission, making them ideal for fee-conscious investors.

Question 98
Which of the following is a benefit of investing in mutual funds?

A. Ability to short sell
B. Lower tax exposure

C. Daily pricing
D. Fixed returns

Correct Answer: C. Daily pricing

Explanation:
Mutual funds are priced once per day, after market close, based on their NAV.

Question 99
A variable life insurance policy allows the policyholder to:

A. Choose from subaccounts to invest the cash value
B. Invest in Treasury bonds only
C. Withdraw without penalty at any time
D. Guarantee a fixed cash value

Correct Answer: A. Choose from subaccounts to invest the cash value

Explanation:
Variable life policies let the owner allocate premiums into separate investment accounts. The cash value and death benefit may fluctuate with performance.

Question 100
Which of the following is not required for mutual fund suitability analysis?

A. Time horizon
B. Investment experience
C. Income verification
D. Investment objectives

Correct Answer: C. Income verification

Explanation:
While income is considered, verification is not mandatory. Reps must collect reasonable data to assess suitability, including time horizon and risk tolerance.

CHAPTER 13
PRACTICE QUESTIONS FOR SERIES 63

100 MULTIPLE-CHOICE QUESTIONS WITH DETAILED EXPLANATIONS

Question 1

Under the Uniform Securities Act (USA), who has authority to issue cease and desist orders?

A. SEC
B. FINRA
C. State Administrator
D. Broker-Dealer

Correct Answer: C. State Administrator

Explanation:

Only the State Administrator has the authority under the USA to issue cease and desist orders when there's a reasonable belief a person is engaging in illegal or unethical securities practices.

Question 2
Which of the following is *not* considered a "security" under the Uniform Securities Act?

A. Stock
B. Investment contract
C. Fixed annuity
D. Debenture

Correct Answer: C. Fixed annuity

Explanation:
Fixed annuities are not classified as securities because they have guaranteed returns and lack investment risk. Variable annuities, however, are securities.

Question 3
A broker-dealer has no office in the state and deals only with institutional clients there. Is registration required?

A. Yes
B. No
C. Only if they advertise online
D. Only if requested by the SEC

Correct Answer: B. No

Explanation:
Under the USA, a broker-dealer with no place of business in the state and who deals exclusively with institutions is not required to register in that state.

Question 4
Which of the following would be considered an "agent" under the USA?

A. A silent partner in a brokerage
B. A secretary who files paperwork
C. An individual selling securities for a broker-dealer
D. A self-directed investor

Correct Answer: C. An individual selling securities for a broker-dealer

Explanation:
An agent is any individual who represents a broker-dealer or issuer in selling securities. Secretarial or clerical staff are not considered agents.

Question 5
Registration under the Uniform Securities Act must be renewed:

A. Every 3 years
B. On the anniversary date of initial registration
C. By December 31 annually
D. Upon request from the SEC

Correct Answer: C. By December 31 annually

Explanation:
All registrations under the USA expire on December 31, regardless of when they were filed during the year. Renewal requires a fee and update of records.

Question 6
Under the USA, which of the following would **not** be required to register as an investment adviser?

A. A lawyer giving incidental advice
B. A firm offering advice on mutual funds for a fee

C. A publisher recommending specific stocks to readers
D. A person advising on securities but charging no fee

Correct Answer: A. A lawyer giving incidental advice

Explanation:
Professionals like lawyers, accountants, and teachers are exempt if their advice is incidental and not compensated separately for investment advice.

Question 7
An agent tells a client, "This investment is guaranteed to double in 12 months." This is:

A. Suitable
B. Allowed for blue-chip stocks
C. Fraudulent
D. Ethical if disclosed in writing

Correct Answer: C. Fraudulent

Explanation:
It is unlawful and unethical to guarantee returns on a security. Such statements are considered misleading and fraudulent under the USA.

Question 8
A client is 75 years old and has a low risk tolerance. Recommending leveraged ETFs may violate which principle?

A. Suitability
B. Liquidity
C. Disclosure
D. Registration

Correct Answer: A. Suitability

Explanation:
Recommending risky, complex products like leveraged ETFs to an elderly client with low risk tolerance violates the suitability standard.

Question 9
Which of the following is required on an agent's registration application?

A. Marital status
B. Personal investment history
C. Disciplinary history
D. Client contact log

Correct Answer: C. Disciplinary history

Explanation:
The application must disclose criminal background, prior regulatory actions, and disciplinary events.

Question 10
When does a state Administrator have the authority to suspend or revoke a registration?

A. Only if the individual is convicted of a felony
B. For any violation, including willful or unintentional
C. Only for violations that cause monetary loss
D. Only after court approval

Correct Answer: B. For any violation, including willful or unintentional

Explanation:
The Administrator may act if an applicant willfully or unknowingly violates provisions of the USA, including failure to supervise or material misstatements.

Question 11
If an agent is terminated, who must notify the Administrator?

A. Only the agent
B. Only the broker-dealer
C. Both the agent and the broker-dealer
D. No one; the registration just lapses

Correct Answer: C. Both the agent and the broker-dealer

Explanation:
The agent and the broker-dealer are jointly responsible for notifying the Administrator when an agent is terminated.

Question 12
An agent steals client funds. This is considered:

A. Unethical but not unlawful
B. Civil misconduct
C. Fraud
D. Negligent supervision

Correct Answer: C. Fraud

Explanation:
Stealing client funds constitutes fraud under both federal and state law. It's a criminal act with serious consequences.

Question 13
A broker-dealer mails a prospectus 10 days after the sale. This is:

A. Permissible
B. A minor violation

C. Prohibited
D. Required by the Administrator

Correct Answer: C. Prohibited

Explanation:
A prospectus must be delivered at or before the confirmation of the transaction. Delayed delivery is a violation of disclosure rules.

Question 14
Under the USA, when must material changes be reported to the Administrator?

A. At year-end
B. Within 30 days
C. Immediately
D. At the next renewal date

Correct Answer: C. Immediately

Explanation:
All material changes (such as a disciplinary action or a change in business location) must be reported promptly or immediately.

Question 15
Which of the following would **not** be considered a "sale" under the USA?

A. A gift of a non-assessable security
B. A gift of an assessable stock
C. A transfer of shares for consideration
D. A bonus with the purchase of a security

Correct Answer: A. A gift of a non-assessable security

Explanation:
A non-assessable stock given as a gift is not a sale, but a gift of an assessable security is considered a sale due to the potential future liability.

Question 16
Which of the following would most likely be a prohibited practice under the USA?

A. Touting a well-diversified fund
B. Recommending based on suitability
C. Failing to disclose a conflict of interest
D. Charging a reasonable commission

Correct Answer: C. Failing to disclose a conflict of interest

Explanation:
Agents and IAs must disclose any conflicts of interest to maintain ethical integrity. Failure to do so is prohibited.

Question 17
An Administrator can require a broker-dealer to:

A. Purchase insurance for all clients
B. Post a surety bond
C. Guarantee investment returns
D. Only hire agents with a Series 7

Correct Answer: B. Post a surety bond

Explanation:
Administrators can require surety bonds to ensure compliance with laws, especially if a firm has custody of client funds.

Question 18
Which of the following must be registered under the USA?

A. US Treasury bonds
B. Commercial paper maturing in 30 days
C. Stock in a public company sold to retail investors
D. Municipal bonds

Correct Answer: C. Stock in a public company sold to retail investors

Explanation:
Stocks sold to the public must be registered, unless they qualify for an exemption. US and municipal securities are usually exempt.

Question 19
An individual is convicted of a securities-related felony. How long must they wait to register?

A. 5 years
B. 10 years
C. 1 year
D. They are permanently barred

Correct Answer: B. 10 years

Explanation:
Anyone convicted of a securities-related felony or misdemeanor in the past 10 years is statutorily disqualified from registration.

Question 20
Who enforces the anti-fraud provisions of the USA?

A. SEC only
B. State Attorney General

C. State Administrator
D. FINRA

Correct Answer: C. State Administrator

Explanation:
While federal regulators may act too, enforcement of state anti-fraud rules falls primarily to the State Administrator.

Question 21
Which of the following is considered a dishonest or unethical business practice under the USA?

A. Telling a client about a new IPO
B. Delaying the delivery of securities for 10 days
C. Recommending securities based on client objectives
D. Charging a fee for preparing a financial plan

Correct Answer: B. Delaying the delivery of securities for 10 days

Explanation:
Delays in delivering securities or funds beyond a reasonable period are considered unethical under the USA.

Question 22
Under the USA, how long must records be maintained by broker-dealers and investment advisers?

A. 3 years
B. 5 years
C. 6 years
D. 7 years

Correct Answer: B. 5 years

Explanation:
Records must be retained for 5 years, and the first 2 years must be in an easily accessible location.

Question 23
If a broker-dealer intentionally omits material facts in a sales presentation, this is considered:

A. Churning
B. Fraud
C. Suitability violation
D. Commingling

Correct Answer: B. Fraud

Explanation:
Omitting material facts is considered a form of fraud, even if the misrepresentation is unintentional. Full disclosure is required.

Question 24
Which of the following would be exempt from registration under the USA?

A. A public offering of common stock
B. A private placement to 50 investors
C. A mutual fund offering
D. A hedge fund sold to accredited investors

Correct Answer: B. A private placement to 50 investors

Explanation:
Private placements to no more than 10 retail investors (institutional unlimited) are generally exempt, provided there's no general advertising or compensation.

Question 25
A client accuses an agent of fraud. Who investigates the matter under state law?

A. SEC
B. FINRA
C. State Administrator
D. State Attorney General

Correct Answer: C. State Administrator

Explanation:
The **Administrator** has the authority to **investigate, subpoena, and take disciplinary action** for violations under the USA.

Question 26
Which of the following may be **legally advertised** without violating the USA?

A. A testimonial from a client
B. A guarantee of performance
C. An explanation of fund objectives
D. A projection of future returns

Correct Answer: C. An explanation of fund objectives

Explanation:
Advertising is allowed if it's truthful and not misleading. Guaranteeing returns or projecting performance is prohibited.

Question 27
What is the statute of limitations for civil suits under the USA?

A. 1 year from the violation
B. 2 years from discovery or 3 years from the violation

C. 5 years from discovery
D. 10 years after registration

Correct Answer: B. 2 years from discovery or 3 years from the violation

Explanation:
Civil suits must be filed within 2 years of discovery of the violation or 3 years from the act, whichever comes first.

Question 28
Which of the following actions would require an investment adviser registration under the USA?

A. Giving free newsletters to friends
B. Giving incidental advice as a teacher
C. Managing portfolios for a fee
D. Making personal investments

Correct Answer: C. Managing portfolios for a fee

Explanation:
Any person who manages portfolios and receives compensation must register as an investment adviser, unless exempt.

Question 29
A guarantee against loss by a representative is:

A. Required for fiduciaries

B. Allowed with principal approval
C. Prohibited under the USA
D. Acceptable if written

Correct Answer: C. Prohibited under the USA

Explanation:
No broker-dealer, agent, or adviser may guarantee performance or protect clients from losses—this is strictly prohibited.

Question 30
Who is considered a federal covered adviser?

A. An adviser with fewer than 5 clients
B. An adviser only working with mutual funds
C. An adviser registered at the state level
D. An adviser managing $50 million in assets

Correct Answer: B. An adviser only working with mutual funds

Explanation:
Advisers who manage registered investment companies (e.g., mutual funds) are federal covered advisers, even if they don't meet the AUM threshold.

Question 31
Which term describes using client funds for personal use?

A. Front-running
B. Commingling
C. Conversion
D. Insider trading

Correct Answer: C. Conversion

Explanation:
Conversion occurs when a rep uses client funds for unauthorized personal use, which is fraudulent and illegal.

Question 32

When must prospectus delivery be made in a registered offering?

A. Before any communication
B. Prior to the purchase
C. Within 24 hours
D. After the confirmation is sent

Correct Answer: B. Prior to the purchase

Explanation:

The prospectus must be delivered at or before the point of sale or transaction to ensure proper disclosure.

Question 33

A broker-dealer's website contains misleading performance data. This is:

A. Permissible if disclaimers are used
B. Subject to FINRA only
C. A violation of USA advertising rules
D. Allowed for institutional investors

Correct Answer: C. A violation of USA advertising rules

Explanation:

All advertising, including websites, must be truthful, balanced, and not misleading. Performance must include disclaimers and context.

Question 34

Which person is considered excluded from the definition of an investment adviser?

A. A person charging fees for securities analysis
B. A CPA giving investment advice as part of tax prep

C. A person managing 401(k) plans for multiple companies
D. A publishing firm recommending stocks to subscribers

Correct Answer: B. A CPA giving investment advice as part of tax prep

Explanation:
Professionals giving incidental advice as part of their primary role (lawyer, CPA, teacher) are excluded from IA definition.

Question 35
What is the maximum civil penalty for a willful violation under the USA?

A. $1,000
B. $5,000
C. $10,000
D. Treble damages

Correct Answer: B. $5,000

Explanation:
Civil penalties under the USA for willful violations do not exceed $5,000 per violation. Criminal penalties differ.

Question 36
When may an Administrator deny registration based solely on lack of experience?

A. Always
B. Never
C. Only if experience is material to the job
D. Only if combined with insufficient net capital

Correct Answer: B. Never

Explanation:
The Administrator may not deny registration solely based on lack of experience if the applicant meets all other requirements.

Question 37
Which of the following must be filed with the Administrator by investment advisers?

A. Advertising directed at institutions
B. Private correspondence
C. General account statements
D. Social media posts to retail clients

Correct Answer: D. Social media posts to retail clients

Explanation:
Any public communication, including retail-targeted social media posts, must often be reviewed or filed depending on content.

Question 38
A state Administrator can summarily suspend a registration:

A. Without a hearing, if public interest is served
B. Only with federal approval
C. Only after a criminal conviction
D. After FINRA notifies them

Correct Answer: A. Without a hearing, if public interest is served

Explanation:
The Administrator may summarily suspend or deny a registration without prior hearing but must promptly notify the registrant.

Question 39
What defines a "sale" under the USA?

A. Only completed transactions
B. A gift of any security
C. Every contract of disposition for value
D. A disclosure document

Correct Answer: C. Every contract of disposition for value

Explanation:
A sale includes any attempt or contract to dispose of a security for value, including bonuses tied to purchases.

Question 40
A representative offers to reimburse a client's loss. This is:

A. Permissible with disclosure
B. A fiduciary gesture
C. Prohibited as a guarantee
D. Common practice

Correct Answer: C. Prohibited as a guarantee

Explanation:
Guaranteeing against loss or reimbursing client losses is prohibited under both federal and state law. It creates misleading expectations.

Question 41
An agent is discussing investments with a prospective client at a dinner party. Which of the following best describes this activity?

A. Institutional solicitation
B. Selling away

C. Solicitation
D. Networking

Correct Answer: C. Solicitation

Explanation:
Any attempt to interest someone in purchasing a security, regardless of the setting, is considered solicitation under the USA and must be done in accordance with registration rules.

Question 42
A state Administrator can deny an application based on:

A. The applicant's political beliefs
B. The applicant's age
C. A securities-related misdemeanor within the past 10 years
D. The applicant failing a college class

Correct Answer: C. A securities-related misdemeanor within the past 10 years

Explanation:
A securities-related misdemeanor or felony within the past 10 years is grounds for denial, suspension, or revocation of registration.

Question 43
An agent cold-calls a prospective client who is listed on the national "Do Not Call" registry. This is:

A. Permissible if the agent discloses their name
B. Permissible only with written permission
C. A violation unless there is an existing business relationship
D. Allowed if the call is made before 9 PM

Correct Answer: C. A violation unless there is an existing business relationship

Explanation:
Cold-calling someone on the "Do Not Call" registry is prohibited unless there is a prior relationship or explicit consent.

Question 44
A registration application is filed on December 15. When does it expire if not renewed?

A. December 15 of the next year
B. Immediately if denied
C. December 31 of the current year
D. 60 days from approval

Correct Answer: C. December 31 of the current year

Explanation:
All registrations under the USA expire annually on December 31, regardless of the filing date.

Question 45
A representative commingles client and firm assets. This practice is:

A. Permissible if authorized by the client
B. Allowed under a joint agreement
C. Strictly prohibited and unethical
D. Regulated by FINRA only

Correct Answer: C. Strictly prohibited and unethical

Explanation:
Commingling client funds with personal or firm assets is strictly prohibited and a serious regulatory violation.

Question 46
A client files a civil complaint about unsuitable recommendations. Which of the following is true?

A. The Administrator must prosecute criminally
B. The client is entitled to the full value of the investment
C. The Administrator may seek restitution
D. The Administrator refers the case to the SEC

Correct Answer: C. The Administrator may seek restitution

Explanation:
For civil matters, the Administrator may pursue restitution to make the client whole but cannot impose criminal penalties.

Question 47
Which of the following is considered a federal covered security?

A. A security listed on a state exchange
B. Securities issued by a registered investment company
C. A small private placement
D. A security exempt from federal registration

Correct Answer: B. Securities issued by a registered investment company

Explanation:
Securities issued by mutual funds or exchange-listed companies are considered federal covered and are exempt from state registration.

Question 48
Which of the following would cause **automatic denial** of registration?

A. Being sued for defamation
B. Filing incomplete paperwork

C. Felony conviction for burglary 8 years ago
D. Having poor credit

Correct Answer: C. Felony conviction for burglary 8 years ago

Explanation:
Any felony conviction or securities-related misdemeanor within 10 years results in automatic denial under the USA.

Question 49
A client loses money due to poor market performance. The agent is liable:

A. Only if the client is elderly
B. If the agent failed to explain risks
C. Never, unless there was fraud
D. Always, due to fiduciary duty

Correct Answer: C. Never, unless there was fraud

Explanation:
Agents are not liable for normal market losses unless there was fraud, misrepresentation, or negligence involved.

Question 50
Under the USA, the term "person" includes:

A. An individual
B. A corporation
C. A government agency
D. All of the above

Correct Answer: D. All of the above

Explanation:
The USA defines "person" broadly to include individuals, partnerships, corporations, associations, and governments.

Question 51
Which of the following is **not** a method of registering a security under the USA?

A. Coordination
B. Filing (Notification)
C. Qualification
D. Certification

Correct Answer: D. Certification

Explanation:
Certification is not a recognized registration method under the USA. The three valid methods are Notification (Filing), Coordination, and Qualification.

Question 52
An investment adviser firm manages $130 million in assets. Where must it register?

A. With the state
B. With the SEC only
C. With FINRA
D. Registration not required

Correct Answer: B. With the SEC only

Explanation:
Advisers with $110 million or more in AUM must register with the SEC. This adviser is a federal covered adviser.

Question 53

An agent promotes an unregistered, non-exempt security to a retail client. This is:

A. Allowed with disclosure
B. Permitted with client consent
C. A violation of state law
D. A standard sales tactic

Correct Answer: C. A violation of state law

Explanation:

It is illegal to offer or sell a non-exempt, unregistered security to the public. This violates both registration and anti-fraud provisions.

Question 54

An Administrator may require that a sales literature filing be made:

A. Only for federally covered securities
B. Only by investment advisers
C. For securities being offered in the state
D. If the material is from the SEC

Correct Answer: C. For securities being offered in the state

Explanation:

If a security is being offered to residents of a state, the Administrator may request review and filing of sales materials.

Question 55

If a customer complains about unauthorized trades, the broker-dealer must:

A. Inform the SEC
B. Submit a Form U4 amendment

C. Investigate and respond to the client
D. Refund all trades automatically

Correct Answer: C. Investigate and respond to the client

Explanation:
Firms must investigate complaints thoroughly and respond to the client in a timely and documented manner.

Question 56
An Administrator can subpoena records:

A. Only if there's proof of wrongdoing
B. With reasonable suspicion of a violation
C. Only with federal approval
D. Only within state boundaries

Correct Answer: B. With reasonable suspicion of a violation

Explanation:
An Administrator may subpoena documents and witnesses during an investigation based on reasonable suspicion, not just proof.

Question 57
Which of the following would be considered commingling?

A. Pooling client and firm funds in a joint account
B. Buying two securities with the same account
C. Keeping client checks in a secure drawer
D. Making identical recommendations to multiple clients

Correct Answer: A. Pooling client and firm funds in a joint account

Explanation:
Commingling occurs when client and firm assets are mixed inappropriately, violating custody and ethical rules.

Question 58
How often must investment advisers update their Form ADV?

A. Quarterly
B. Every two years
C. Annually, within 90 days of fiscal year-end
D. Only upon material changes

Correct Answer: C. Annually, within 90 days of fiscal year-end

Explanation:
Form ADV must be updated annually and filed within 90 days of the end of the adviser's fiscal year.

Question 59
A client's financial objective changes. The adviser should:

A. Do nothing until asked
B. Immediately update the suitability profile
C. Close the account
D. Require the client to submit a written affidavit

Correct Answer: B. Immediately update the suitability profile

Explanation:
Advisers and reps must maintain current client information. A change in objectives requires reassessment of recommendations.

Question 60
Who must sign a consent to service of process?

A. Clients
B. State regulators
C. All registrants
D. The Administrator only

Correct Answer: C. All registrants

Explanation:
All individuals or firms registering under the USA must sign a consent to service of process, allowing legal documents to be sent via the Administrator.

Question 61
Which of the following is a requirement for an investment adviser representative (IAR) registration in a state?

A. They must have a CFP designation
B. They must live in the state
C. They must have a sponsoring investment adviser
D. They must be affiliated with a federal covered adviser only

Correct Answer: C. They must have a sponsoring investment adviser

Explanation:
An IAR must be employed or affiliated with a registered investment adviser (state or federal) to register in a state.

Question 62
Which of the following securities would most likely be **exempt from state registration**?

A. Preferred stock of a private corporation
B. Bonds issued by a church
C. Municipal bonds issued by another state
D. A real estate investment trust (REIT)

Correct Answer: C. Municipal bonds issued by another state

Explanation:
Municipal securities, regardless of state, are generally exempt from registration under both federal and state law.

Question 63
Under the USA, the term "issuer" applies to:

A. A person offering to buy securities
B. The person offering securities for sale
C. The investment adviser
D. A mutual fund shareholder

Correct Answer: B. The person offering securities for sale

Explanation:
An issuer is defined as the entity or person proposing to issue or distribute a security to the public.

Question 64
Which of the following would most likely result in statutory disqualification?

A. A civil lawsuit for negligence
B. Being the subject of a customer complaint
C. A felony conviction involving theft
D. A failed Series 63 exam

Correct Answer: C. A felony conviction involving theft

Explanation:
Felonies or securities-related misdemeanors within the past 10 years cause statutory disqualification.

Question 65
Which of the following business entities **must** register as a broker-dealer under the USA?

A. A firm that only provides investment research
B. A firm buying and selling securities for client accounts
C. A non-profit company managing pension plans
D. A company investing only in its own securities

Correct Answer: B. A firm buying and selling securities for client accounts

Explanation:
Any firm executing securities transactions for others must register as a broker-dealer unless exempt.

Question 66
Which of the following transactions is not considered a sale under the Uniform Securities Act?

A. A bonus security given with purchase
B. A stock dividend
C. A gift of assessable stock
D. A security transferred for cash

Correct Answer: B. A stock dividend

Explanation:
Stock dividends are not considered sales since they are given without consideration (payment).

Question 67

An agent falsely tells a client that a security is registered with the Administrator. This is:

A. Acceptable as long as the security is legitimate
B. Acceptable if the client requests it
C. Prohibited because it implies approval
D. Required to sell the security

Correct Answer: C. Prohibited because it implies approval

Explanation:

Claiming that registration implies approval or endorsement is prohibited under the USA.

Question 68

If a firm goes out of business, how long must its records be maintained?

A. 1 year
B. 3 years
C. 5 years
D. 6 years

Correct Answer: C. 5 years

Explanation:

Records must still be maintained for 5 years after the firm ceases operations.

Question 69

An agent shares client information with a friend. This is:

A. Acceptable if no harm occurs
B. A breach of privacy and ethics

C. Legal if the client doesn't object
D. Required for transparency

Correct Answer: B. A breach of privacy and ethics

Explanation:
Agents have a duty to protect client confidentiality. Sharing data without consent is a serious violation.

Question 70
An Administrator may deny a registration based on:

A. A minor speeding ticket
B. An agent's religion
C. Lack of experience and insolvency
D. Willful violation of state rules

Correct Answer: D. Willful violation of state rules

Explanation:
The Administrator can act on willful violations or misleading omissions, but not on unrelated personal details.

Question 71
A client wants to trade options, but the rep never explains the risks. This is:

A. An example of due diligence
B. Permissible if the trade is profitable
C. A violation of suitability and disclosure rules
D. Fine if the client is wealthy

Correct Answer: C. A violation of suitability and disclosure rules

Explanation:
Reps must explain complex investment risks like options before trading. Failure is a violation.

Question 72
An Administrator wants to deny registration due to a felony charge. What must exist?

A. A conviction
B. An indictment
C. A written warning
D. A FINRA suspension

Correct Answer: A. A conviction

Explanation:
The Administrator may only deny registration based on a conviction, not merely an accusation or indictment.

Question 73
Under the USA, who is responsible for updating a representative's Form U4?

A. FINRA
B. The representative
C. The employer (BD or IA)
D. The client

Correct Answer: C. The employer (BD or IA)

Explanation:
Employers are responsible for filing and updating Form U4 for all registered personnel.

Question 74
Which of the following is a prohibited activity?

A. Recommending a diversified portfolio
B. Omitting material facts
C. Explaining risk tolerance
D. Offering a research report

Correct Answer: B. Omitting material facts

Explanation:
Omission of material facts is treated the same as misrepresentation and is considered fraudulent.

Question 75
A broker-dealer accepts payment but never delivers the security. This is:

A. A minor paperwork error
B. A failure to supervise
C. A dishonest and unethical business practice
D. Permissible if refunded quickly

Correct Answer: C. A dishonest and unethical business practice

Explanation:
Failing to deliver securities or funds in a reasonable time is explicitly listed as unethical under the USA.

Question 76
An Administrator denies a registration. The applicant may:

A. Ignore the decision
B. Appeal to the state Attorney General

C. Request a hearing within 60 days
D. Request a hearing within 30 days

Correct Answer: D. Request a hearing within 30 days

Explanation:
The registrant must request a hearing within 30 days of receiving notice of the Administrator's action.

Question 77
Under the USA, a firm with custody of client funds must:

A. Provide monthly statements

B. Maintain a minimum net capital
C. Be SEC registered
D. Operate under a depository trust

Correct Answer: B. Maintain a minimum net capital

Explanation:
Firms with custody are subject to net capital and bonding requirements to ensure financial strength.

Question 78
Which of the following would most likely require registration as a broker-dealer?

A. A person selling securities to family members
B. An individual with a self-directed IRA
C. A company buying and selling for others
D. A charity selling endowment investments

Correct Answer: C. A company buying and selling for others

Explanation:
If you're engaged in the business of buying and selling securities for others, you're considered a broker-dealer.

Question 79
Which of the following is **not** a valid disciplinary action under the USA?

A. Censure
B. Suspension
C. Fines
D. Forced arbitration

Correct Answer: D. Forced arbitration

Explanation:
The Administrator can suspend, revoke, or censure, but cannot require arbitration unless agreed upon in advance.

Question 80
A sales pitch implies a state has approved the investment. This is:

A. An ethical disclosure
B. A requirement
C. A violation
D. A sales tool

Correct Answer: C. A violation

Explanation:
Saying a state "approved" an offering is prohibited. Registration does not imply approval by regulators.

Question 81

Which of the following is **true** regarding an investment adviser's brochure (ADV Part 2)?

A. It must include past performance returns
B. It is only required for federal covered advisers
C. It must be given to clients no later than 48 hours before entering a contract
D. It is optional if the client is institutional

Correct Answer: C. It must be given to clients no later than 48 hours before entering a contract

Explanation:

Under the USA, advisers must deliver Form ADV Part 2 (the brochure) 48 hours prior to contract signing or at signing with a 5-day withdrawal right.

Question 82

If an agent resigns from a firm, who must notify the Administrator?

A. The agent only
B. The agent and the Administrator
C. The broker-dealer only
D. Both the agent and the broker-dealer

Correct Answer: D. Both the agent and the broker-dealer

Explanation:

When an agent terminates employment, both the agent and the broker-dealer must notify the state Administrator promptly.

Question 83

An agent wants to share in profits and losses with a client. When is this permitted?

A. If the agent has written approval from the Administrator
B. Only if the agent contributes proportionally to the account
C. If FINRA approves it
D. Always, if disclosed verbally

Correct Answer: B. Only if the agent contributes proportionally to the account

Explanation:

Agents may share profits/losses only with written client consent and proportional capital contribution.

Question 84

An agent uses material inside information in a trade. What is the most likely consequence?

A. No action unless the client complains
B. Fine but no jail time
C. Civil and criminal penalties, including imprisonment
D. Required arbitration

Correct Answer: C. Civil and criminal penalties, including imprisonment

Explanation:

Insider trading is a criminal offense punishable by fines, jail, and civil liability under federal and state law.

Question 85
What does the term "offer to sell" include under the Uniform Securities Act?

A. Every verbal recommendation
B. Only completed transactions
C. An attempt to dispose of a security for value
D. A public filing of financial statements

Correct Answer: C. An attempt to dispose of a security for value

Explanation:

An "offer to sell" includes any attempt to dispose of a security or solicitation for value, even if a sale doesn't occur.

Question 86
Which of the following would be excluded from the definition of a broker-dealer?

A. A person effecting trades for others
B. An individual making personal trades
C. A firm handling trades for the public
D. An entity compensated for selling securities

Correct Answer: B. An individual making personal trades

Explanation:
A person who buys and sells solely for personal investment is not a broker-dealer under the USA.

Question 87
An adviser with no office in a state gives advice to 4 clients there. Must they register?

A. Yes, always
B. No, the de minimis exemption applies
C. Only if advising institutions
D. Only after receiving compensation

Correct Answer: B. No, the de minimis exemption applies

Explanation:
The de minimis exemption applies to advisers with no office in the state and five or fewer non-institutional clients in 12 months.

Question 88
An Administrator issues a cease and desist order. What must they also do?

A. Give the person 15 days' notice
B. Immediately revoke registration
C. Grant a hearing if requested
D. Notify the SEC

Correct Answer: C. Grant a hearing if requested

Explanation:
While a cease and desist order can be issued without a hearing, the subject may request a hearing, which must be granted within 15 days.

Question 89
What is the primary purpose of the Uniform Securities Act?

A. Protect agents from liability
B. Provide investment recommendations
C. Prevent and penalize fraud in securities transactions
D. Regulate the federal market

Correct Answer: C. Prevent and penalize fraud in securities transactions

Explanation:
The USA exists primarily to protect investors by preventing fraudulent, deceptive, and manipulative practices.

Question 90
Which of the following would be considered a **material fact**?

A. The firm changed its logo
B. The client is opening a new account
C. The company is facing a large lawsuit
D. The market is up 10% this year

Correct Answer: C. The company is facing a large lawsuit

Explanation:
Material facts include anything that would influence an investor's decision, such as pending lawsuits or financial instability.

Question 91
An agent recommends excessive trading to generate commissions. This is called:

A. Front-running
B. Churning
C. Switching
D. Misappropriation

Correct Answer: B. Churning

Explanation:
Churning refers to excessive trading in a client's account to generate commissions, which violates fiduciary obligations.

Question 92

Which of the following is **not** a defined security under the USA?

A. Investment contract
B. Voting trust certificate
C. Fixed annuity
D. Debenture

Correct Answer: C. Fixed annuity

Explanation:

Fixed annuities are not considered securities, as they are insurance products with no investment risk.

Question 93

An IAR receives a verbal complaint from a client. What is the required action?

A. Report it to FINRA
B. Document it internally
C. Ignore unless in writing
D. Notify the SEC

Correct Answer: C. Ignore unless in writing

Explanation:

Only written complaints must be reported and retained. However, it's best practice to document all complaints internally.

Question 94

A firm fails to deliver securities and is fined. What kind of action is this?

A. Civil
B. Regulatory

C. Arbitration
D. Criminal

Correct Answer: A. Civil

Explanation:
Fines and restitution in such cases fall under civil liability, not criminal or regulatory suspension.

Question 95
What type of client is not counted against the de minimis exemption?

A. An accredited investor
B. An institutional client
C. A retail client with $10 million
D. A non-resident

Correct Answer: B. An institutional client

Explanation:
Institutional clients are not counted toward the 5-client threshold of the de minimis rule.

Question 96
Who must register as an agent under the USA?

A. A silent partner in a BD
B. An individual selling securities for a BD
C. An admin assistant answering phones
D. A mutual fund shareholder

Correct Answer: B. An individual selling securities for a BD

Explanation:
Anyone effecting securities transactions on behalf of a broker-dealer must register as an agent.

Question 97
Which of the following is considered **fraudulent** under the USA?

A. Omission of non-material facts
B. Guaranteeing a return
C. Failing to offer quarterly statements
D. Receiving trail commissions

Correct Answer: B. Guaranteeing a return

Explanation:
Guarantees of investment performance are fraudulent and prohibited. All investments carry risk.

Question 98
A client signs a waiver of rights under the USA. What is the status of that waiver?

A. Valid only if notarized
B. Binding upon mutual agreement
C. Void and unenforceable
D. Valid with Administrator approval

Correct Answer: C. Void and unenforceable

Explanation:
Any clause that waives compliance with the USA is void. Investor protections cannot be signed away.

Question 99

An Administrator may inspect a registrant's books:

A. Once a year
B. Only with a court order
C. Without notice if in the public interest
D. Never if federally registered

Correct Answer: C. Without notice if in the public interest

Explanation:

The Administrator may inspect records without prior notice to protect the public interest.

Question 100

A broker-dealer with no office in the state executes trades with 3 retail clients in that state. What is required?

A. State registration as a BD
B. No registration needed
C. Federal notice filing
D. SEC approval

Correct Answer: A. State registration as a BD

Explanation:

A broker-dealer must register in a state if it has even one retail client there, unless exempt by the USA.

CHAPTER 14
FULL-LENGTH PRACTICE EXAMS

Simulated Series 6 Exam
50 Multiple-Choice Questions
Time Limit: 90 minutes
Passing Score: 70% (35 correct answers)

Instructions:

- Each question has one correct answer.
- Do not reference notes during the test—treat it like a real exam.
- After completing all 50 questions, refer to the answer key with detailed explanations provided at the end of the test.

Question 1
Which of the following securities can a Series 6 representative sell?

A. Individual stocks
B. Exchange-traded funds (ETFs)
C. Unit Investment Trusts (UITs)
D. Options on mutual funds

Question 2

An investor receives a prospectus after purchasing mutual fund shares. This is:

A. A violation of SEC delivery rules
B. Permitted if within 5 business days
C. Permitted if the purchase was unsolicited
D. A violation unless the fund is closed-end

Question 3

An investor in a mutual fund is subject to capital gains distributions. These are:

A. Not taxable if reinvested
B. Taxable only when withdrawn
C. Taxable in the year distributed, even if reinvested
D. Tax-exempt under IRS rules

Question 4

What is the primary function of the transfer agent of a mutual fund?

A. Manage the fund's portfolio
B. Sell fund shares to the public
C. Issue and cancel share certificates
D. Underwrite the fund's IPO

Question 5

An investor buys Class A mutual fund shares. Which of the following is true?

A. They carry 12b-1 fees
B. They have back-end loads
C. They typically charge a front-end sales load
D. They have no loads or expenses

Question 6

Under FINRA rules, all the following must be disclosed in a mutual fund prospectus except:

A. Sales loads
B. Past performance
C. Fund manager's social media
D. Investment objectives

Question 7

Which of the following is an example of non-systematic risk?

A. Market crash
B. Recession
C. Business failure due to fraud
D. Inflation surge

Question 8

The price at which a mutual fund shareholder can redeem their shares is:

A. The ask price
B. The net asset value (NAV)
C. The public offering price (POP)
D. The market price

Question 9

Which of the following actions by a registered rep is permitted?

A. Guaranteeing a mutual fund will outperform the index
B. Recommending mutual fund share classes based on client profile
C. Offering a client a rebate of part of the sales charge
D. Telling a client the NAV will rise tomorrow

Question 10

A 529 college savings plan allows:

A. Contributions limited to $1,000 per year
B. Tax-free distributions for qualified education expenses
C. Penalty-free withdrawals for any reason
D. Unlimited investment options

Question 11

Which of the following would result in a letter of intent (LOI) being canceled?

A. Client redeems shares before completing LOI
B. Client signs a new LOI
C. NAV drops below intended breakpoint
D. Client changes address

Question 12

What happens if an investor fails to complete the LOI within the time frame?

A. Nothing
B. They lose all their shares
C. The sales charge is recalculated retroactively
D. The fund issues a warning

Question 13

Which of the following is not a redeemable security?

A. Mutual fund share
B. UIT unit
C. Closed-end fund
D. Variable annuity

Question 14

A client is most concerned about purchasing power risk. You should recommend:

A. A long-term bond fund
B. A savings account
C. A growth mutual fund
D. A money market account

Question 15

The **custodian** of a mutual fund is responsible for:

A. Registering the fund with the SEC
B. Holding the fund's securities
C. Selling shares to the public
D. Creating investment objectives

Question 16

An investor owns 300 shares of a mutual fund at a NAV of $10. The NAV increases to $12. What is the unrealized gain?

A. $300
B. $600
C. $3,600
D. $4,200

Question 17

Which of the following is true regarding 403(b) plans?

A. They are for military employees only
B. They are funded with after-tax dollars
C. They are tax-deferred retirement plans
D. They have no early withdrawal penalty

Question 18

Which of the following is a **non-qualified** retirement plan?

A. Traditional IRA
B. Roth IRA
C. 401(k)
D. Deferred compensation plan

Question 19

An investor changes their allocation in a variable annuity. This is:

A. A taxable event
B. A prohibited activity
C. A tax-deferred activity
D. Not permitted without SEC approval

Question 20

Which of the following **does not** affect a mutual fund's NAV?

A. Change in value of portfolio securities
B. Payment of fund expenses
C. Redemption of shares
D. Purchase of new shares

Question 21

An agent's recommendation must be:

A. Suitable based on market trends
B. Suitable based on the customer's needs
C. Suitable based on the firm's quarterly target
D. Based on other clients' returns

Question 22
Which of the following is not required to open a mutual fund account?

A. Social Security number
B. Employment information
C. Investment objectives
D. Mother's maiden name

Question 23
Which of the following is a feature of a variable annuity, not a mutual fund?

A. Tax-deferred growth
B. Professionally managed portfolios
C. Guaranteed minimum death benefit
D. Access to NAV at all times

Question 24
Which document explains the mutual fund's goals, strategies, risks, and costs?

A. Fund letter
B. Offering circular
C. Summary prospectus
D. Margin agreement

Question 25
A mutual fund may charge a 12b-1 fee to cover:

A. Advisory services
B. Sales and marketing expenses
C. Custodial services
D. Legal costs related to lawsuits

Question 26

A mutual fund's POP is $10.70 and its NAV is $10.00. What is the sales charge percentage?

A. 5%
B. 6%
C. 7%
D. 7.5%

Question 27

A rep tells a client, "This fund has done well for 5 years—it's guaranteed to continue." This is:

A. Acceptable if the client agrees
B. Acceptable if the fund is high quality
C. Misleading and prohibited
D. Accurate but requires a disclaimer

Question 28

Which of the following would **most** likely reduce a mutual fund's NAV?

A. Redemption of shares
B. Capital gain distribution
C. Investor deposits
D. New fund manager hired

Question 29

A mutual fund can legally delay redemption payments for:

A. 2 business days
B. 5 business days
C. 7 calendar days
D. 10 business days

Question 30

Which of the following accounts is most appropriate for a couple saving for retirement?

A. 403(b)
B. Margin account
C. IRA
D. Education savings account

Question 31

The SEC's Rule 498 governs:

A. Variable annuity registration
B. Fund management turnover
C. Summary prospectus delivery
D. Sales charges on closed-end funds

Question 32

The back-end load on Class B mutual fund shares:

A. Increases over time
B. Remains level throughout ownership
C. Decreases over time
D. Is applied only if the client profits

Question 33

A rep must update their Form U4 if:

A. The client's portfolio declines
B. They switch mutual fund companies
C. They are convicted of a misdemeanor
D. They are arrested for a felony

Question 34
Which of the following would not be suitable for a conservative investor?

A. Government bond fund

B. Balanced mutual fund
C. Growth mutual fund
D. High-yield bond fund

Question 35
FINRA rules require firms to maintain records of mutual fund transactions for:

A. 2 years
B. 3 years
C. 6 years
D. Lifetime of the account

Question 36
Which of the following best describes the purpose of breakpoints?

A. To limit investment risk
B. To create separate fund share classes
C. To reduce sales charges on larger purchases
D. To prevent excessive trading

Question 37
A transfer of assets from one IRA to another must be completed within:

A. 30 days
B. 45 days
C. 60 days
D. 90 days

Question 38

Which type of risk is most closely associated with bond mutual funds?

A. Liquidity risk

B. Credit risk
C. Currency risk
D. Reinvestment risk

Question 39

Which of the following is true regarding mutual fund taxation?

A. All distributions are tax-free
B. Reinvested dividends are not taxable
C. Qualified dividends may be taxed at lower rates
D. Unrealized gains are taxed annually

Question 40

What does a fund family allow investors to do?

A. Purchase stocks and options
B. Switch funds without charge or penalty
C. Move between funds under one sponsor
D. Avoid all sales charges permanently

Question 41

When must a mutual fund investor receive a prospectus?

A. Within 3 business days after purchase
B. Within 5 calendar days
C. Before or at the time of confirmation
D. Before the first dividend is paid

Question 42
Which of the following is a feature of a qualified retirement plan?

A. Contributions are after-tax
B. Distributions are always tax-free
C. Contributions reduce taxable income
D. There is no contribution limit

Question 43
The expense ratio of a fund includes:

A. Sales loads and commissions
B. Operating expenses and management fees
C. Only SEC filing fees
D. Capital gains

Question 44
Which of the following best describes dollar-cost averaging?

A. Buying fewer shares at higher prices
B. Timing the market for best prices
C. Investing a fixed amount regularly regardless of price
D. Making a lump-sum investment

Question 45
An investor rolls over assets from a 401(k) to a traditional IRA. This is:

A. Taxable
B. A prohibited transaction
C. Tax-deferred
D. Tax-free

Question 46
Which of the following would be least likely found in a mutual fund's Statement of Additional Information (SAI)?

A. Portfolio holdings

B. Fee schedules
C. Details on fund managers
D. Daily NAV updates

Question 47
If a client asks for a fund's SAI, the firm must deliver it within:

A. 3 days
B. 5 business days
C. 7 calendar days
D. 10 business days

Question 48
Which share class is best for a long-term investor with a large sum?

A. Class A
B. Class B
C. Class C
D. No-load

Question 49
Which of the following best describes liquidity?

A. Market volatility
B. Speed of converting an asset to cash
C. Yield earned on a bond
D. Leverage potential of an investment

Question 50

A mutual fund's NAV is calculated:

A. Hourly
B. Daily, based on market close
C. Weekly
D. Monthly, after board review

SIMULATED SERIES 6 EXAM – ANSWER KEY & EXPLANATIONS

QUESTIONS 1–50

1. C – Series 6 reps may sell packaged products like mutual funds, UITs, and variable products, not individual stocks or options.
2. A – A prospectus must be delivered at or before the sale; delivering it afterward violates SEC rules.
3. C – Capital gains distributions are taxable in the year distributed, even if automatically reinvested.
4. C – The transfer agent handles share issuance, cancellation, and recordkeeping.
5. C – Class A shares typically carry front-end loads.
6. C – A fund manager's social media is not required in the prospectus.
7. C – Business failure is a non-systematic (company-specific) risk.
8. B – Mutual fund redemptions are paid at the next calculated NAV.
9. B – Suitability-based recommendations are permitted; guarantees or rebates are not.
10. B – Qualified distributions from 529 plans are tax-free if used for approved education expenses.
11. A – Redeeming shares before completing an LOI will void the LOI and retroactively charge full sales load.
12. C – If not completed in 13 months, full sales charges apply retroactively.

13. C – Closed-end funds are traded like stocks; not redeemable with the issuer.
14. C – Growth funds historically beat inflation, protecting purchasing power.
15. B – The custodian safe keeps the fund's assets (e.g., stocks, bonds).
16. B – Gain = (12 – 10) × 300 = $600.
17. C – 403(b) plans are tax-deferred retirement accounts.
18. D – Deferred compensation plans are non-qualified.
19. C – Changes in variable annuity allocation are not taxable events.
20. D – Buying new shares does not affect NAV (only the number of shares outstanding increases).
21. B – Recommendations must be based on the customer's individual needs.
22. D – Mother's maiden name is not required for opening an account.
23. C – Only variable annuities offer guaranteed death benefits.
24. C – The summary prospectus provides key fund info.
25. B – 12b-1 fees cover distribution and marketing expenses.
26. B – Sales charge = (POP – NAV) ÷ POP = (10.70 – 10) ÷ 10.70 ≈ 6.54%, closest to 6%.
27. C – Guaranteeing performance is misleading and prohibited.
28. B – When funds distribute gains, NAV decreases by that amount.
29. C – Redemption payments may be delayed up to 7 calendar days.
30. C – An IRA is a personal retirement plan for individuals or couples.
31. C – Rule 498 governs summary prospectus delivery.
32. C – Class B share back-end loads decrease over time, typically disappearing after 5–7 years.
33. D – Felony arrests and convictions must be disclosed on Form U4.
34. D – High-yield bond funds are riskier, not ideal for conservative clients.
35. C – Most account records are kept for 6 years under FINRA rules.
36. C – Breakpoints give reduced sales charges for larger investments.
37. C – Rollover must be completed within 60 days to avoid taxation.

38. D – Bond funds carry reinvestment risk, especially in falling interest rate environments.
39. C – Qualified dividends may be taxed at lower capital gains rates.
40. C – Fund families allow exchanges within the family, usually without sales charges.
41. C – Prospectuses must be delivered before or with the confirmation.
42. C – Qualified plans allow pre-tax contributions, lowering taxable income.
43. B – Operating costs and advisory fees make up the expense ratio.
44. C – Dollar-cost averaging is systematic investing regardless of price.
45. C – A rollover from a 401(k) to an IRA is tax-deferred.
46. D – Daily NAV info is not in the SAI; it's available elsewhere (e.g., online).
47. C – Firms must deliver the SAI within 7 calendar days of request.
48. A – Class A shares are best for long-term, large investors due to breakpoints and lower annual expenses.
49. B – Liquidity refers to ease of converting to cash without losing value.
50. B – Mutual funds calculate NAV daily after market close (4 PM ET).

PERFORMANCE GUIDE

Score	Rating	Recommendation
45–50	Excellent	Ready for real exam
40–44	Good	Review weak areas
35–39	Borderline	Additional study recommended
<35	Needs Improvement	Review all chapters thoroughly

SIMULATED SERIES 63 EXAM

Instructions:

- Choose the best answer for each question.
- After all 65 questions, you'll receive a complete answer key with detailed explanations.

Question 1

Under the Uniform Securities Act (USA), an agent of a broker-dealer is required to register in a state when:

A. They conduct business exclusively with institutional investors
B. They are employed by a federally covered advisor
C. They sell securities to retail clients in the state
D. They reside in the state, regardless of client location

Question 2

Which of the following is **not** a security under the Uniform Securities Act?

A. A variable annuity
B. A futures contract on wheat
C. A limited partnership interest
D. A preorganization certificate

Question 3

An investment adviser representative (IAR) must register in a state when:

A. They give general economic commentary online
B. They manage client portfolios in that state
C. They are supervised by a federally covered adviser
D. Their clients are institutional only

Question 4

Which of the following would **not** be considered unethical conduct by an agent?

A. Recommending a mutual fund without discussing risks
B. Guaranteeing a client will not lose money
C. Charging a commission disclosed in advance
D. Selling unregistered, non-exempt securities

Question 5

An Administrator has authority to:

A. Levy criminal penalties for fraud
B. File civil suits in federal court
C. Issue subpoenas to compel testimony
D. Enact federal anti-fraud legislation

Question 6

Which of the following is a federally covered security?

A. A security listed on the NYSE
B. A municipal bond issued within the state
C. A private placement under Rule 506(b)
D. All of the above

Question 7

A consent to service of process allows the Administrator to:

A. Audit the broker-dealer's financials
B. Appoint a legal representative for the registrant
C. Seize a client's account for tax evasion
D. Review employment contracts of IARs

Question 8

An agent is working in State A and accidentally solicits a client in State B. The Administrator in State B:

A. Has no authority unless a complaint is filed
B. Can enforce cease and desist orders
C. Can only notify State A's Administrator
D. Must report to the SEC for enforcement

Question 9

Which of the following would most likely be exempt from registration under the USA?

A. A small IPO of a tech company
B. A security issued by a Canadian government
C. A hedge fund sold to retail investors
D. A limited partnership offered across multiple states

Question 10

A customer requests to hold mail while traveling. The firm may:

A. Deny the request
B. Hold the mail for up to 3 months with written instructions
C. Forward mail to another state
D. Disclose this request to the SEC

Question 11

Which of the following is **not** considered an unethical business practice?

A. Commingling client and firm funds
B. Making exaggerated claims about returns
C. Recommending suitable investments
D. Failing to disclose conflicts of interest

Question 12

Under the USA, a private placement exemption requires:

A. Offers to no more than 35 non-institutional clients
B. No commissions to be paid
C. The issuer to register in every state
D. The securities to be exchange-listed

Question 13

Which of the following individuals is not considered an agent?

A. A secretary sending new account forms
B. A rep selling exempt securities to retail clients
C. A person effecting trades for compensation
D. A trainee executing sales under supervision

Question 14

A broker-dealer with no office in a state and who transacts only with banks and insurance companies in that state:

A. Must register in the state
B. Is exempt from registration
C. May only register with the SEC
D. Must register as an IAR

Question 15

An agent wants to share in profits/losses of a customer's account. This is permitted if:

A. The agent has verbal approval from the client
B. The client is an institutional investor
C. The firm and the customer provide written consent
D. It is a joint account with equal funding

Question 16
An IAR moves to a new state. Who is responsible for notifying the Administrator?

A. The IAR
B. The investment adviser
C. The SEC
D. The custodian bank

Question 17
Which of the following is true about surety bonds?

A. They are only required for federally covered advisers
B. They protect clients against fraud
C. They are required even when advisers have custody
D. They are provided by the SIPC

Question 18
A client asks you to purchase a security that is not registered in your state. You should:

A. Place the order immediately
B. Notify the client it is illegal
C. Execute the order only if exempt or federally covered
D. Refer the client to another firm

Question 19
The Administrator's authority to deny registration includes:

A. Previous misdemeanors
B. Felony conviction within the last 10 years
C. Bankruptcy 15 years ago
D. SEC approval of employment history

Question 20

A client buys a non-exempt security that was sold without registration. The client may:

A. File a civil suit to rescind the transaction
B. Receive punitive damages
C. Sue the SEC
D. Demand criminal prosecution

Question 21

If a client dies, the agent should:

A. Liquidate all positions
B. Transfer assets to the beneficiary
C. Mark the account deceased and await instructions
D. Continue placing trades with the executor's consent

Question 22

An agent may not engage in which of the following?

A. Discussing tax strategies
B. Recommending a security
C. Charging a fair commission
D. Borrowing money from a retail client

Question 23

A state Administrator can revoke a securities exemption:

A. At any time, with or without notice
B. Only if fraud is suspected
C. By rule or order, with notice and opportunity for hearing
D. With SEC approval

Question 24
An investment adviser must disclose all of the following except:

A. Methods of analysis
B. Potential conflicts of interest
C. Commission schedules of third-party funds
D. Education background of receptionists

Question 25
An IAR tells a client, "I've personally invested in this fund, so I know it will work." This is:

A. Prohibited, as it implies a guarantee
B. Acceptable if the client agrees
C. Required under fiduciary standards
D. Encouraged under NASAA guidelines

Question 26
An investment adviser with custody of client assets must:

A. Submit to annual FINRA audits
B. Notify clients within 30 days
C. Be audited annually and maintain minimum net worth
D. Avoid using third-party custodians

Question 27
Which of the following is not required in the investment adviser's brochure?

A. Fees and compensation
B. Adviser's social media presence
C. Methods of analysis and investment strategies
D. Disciplinary information

Question 28

A client sues an agent for a securities violation. What is the statute of limitations for civil liability under the USA?

A. 1 year from the violation
B. 2 years from discovery or 3 years from violation
C. 5 years from date of discovery
D. 10 years from the trade

Question 29

Which of the following requires registration in a state?

A. U.S. Treasury bills
B. Municipal bonds issued within the state
C. Variable annuities
D. Commercial paper maturing in 60 days

Question 30

An Administrator may require a broker-dealer to:

A. Post a surety bond if holding client funds
B. Have a minimum of 10 years of experience
C. Employ at least 5 agents
D. Offer 24/7 client services

Question 31

An agent offers to sell a non-exempt security without registration. This is:

A. Permitted if the client is institutional
B. Prohibited unless an exemption applies
C. Acceptable for IPOs only
D. Not covered under the USA

Question 32

An IAR who sends a monthly newsletter to clients must:

A. Avoid any mention of performance
B. File it with the Administrator if it contains specific recommendations
C. Limit it to 3 pages
D. Not mention securities under any circumstances

Question 33

Which of the following is a prohibited practice?

A. Recommending the same security to multiple clients
B. Making recommendations based on financial profiles
C. Omitting material facts
D. Using past performance charts

Question 34

A broker-dealer advertises a guaranteed return on mutual funds. This is:

A. Permissible with disclosure
B. Misleading and prohibited
C. Acceptable under NASAA rules
D. Permitted for Class A shares only

Question 35

Which of the following is true regarding a cease and desist order?

A. It can only be issued after a hearing
B. It is used to enforce federal securities laws
C. It may be issued without prior hearing
D. It replaces civil litigation

Question 36

A firm using soft dollars must ensure:

A. Clients are not informed

B. The services received benefit the adviser's business

C. The services benefit clients and comply with Section 28(e)

D. The adviser charges extra fees

Question 37

An IAR managing portfolios must have discretion authorized by:

A. Verbal confirmation from the client

B. A written power of attorney

C. Oral agreement witnessed by another agent

D. Administrator's approval

Question 38

Which of the following statements is true regarding investment adviser registration?

A. Federal registration exempts them from all state laws

B. All advisers must register with both SEC and states

C. Advisers with over $110 million AUM must register federally

D. State-registered advisers are exempt from SEC audits

Question 39

A registration becomes effective under the USA:

A. Upon Administrator's verbal approval

B. 15 days after filing

C. 30 days after filing, if not denied

D. 90 days after the fiscal year

Question 40

An IAR wants to publish testimonials on their website. This is:

A. Permitted only if anonymous
B. Prohibited under NASAA rules
C. Allowed if compliant with SEC marketing rule and disclosures
D. Allowed only for institutional clients

Question 41

When can an Administrator suspend a registration without prior hearing?

A. Never
B. Only with SEC approval
C. If it is in the public interest and a violation has occurred
D. Only after 30 days' notice

Question 42

An agent opens a joint account with a client. This is allowed if:

A. The client is a family member
B. The agent is a fiduciary
C. Both parties agree in writing
D. It's supervised by FINRA

Question 43

Which of the following securities is exempt from registration under the USA?

A. A mutual fund share
B. A U.S. government bond
C. An oil and gas partnership
D. A foreign corporate bond

Question 44

An IAR preparing to retire recommends all clients switch to annuities. This could be:

A. A prudent practice
B. An example of churning
C. A violation of fiduciary duty due to blanket recommendations
D. A disclosure-only issue

Question 45

Which of the following would not be considered a material change requiring brochure update?

A. A change in advisory fees
B. The addition of a new custodian
C. A receptionist quitting
D. The firm merging with another adviser

Question 46

If a customer sues under the USA and wins, the client may recover:

A. Triple damages and fees
B. The original investment plus interest, costs, and attorney's fees
C. Double the losses only
D. Punitive damages for fraud

Question 47

An agent wants to participate in a private securities transaction. They must:

A. Notify their firm in writing and receive approval
B. Only notify the Administrator
C. File with the SEC
D. Never do this—it's always prohibited

Question 48

The Administrator can deny registration for which of the following reasons?

A. Failure to pay a registration fee
B. Firm does not operate 5 days a week
C. Client losses due to market risk
D. Use of social media by an IAR

Question 49

An agent uses their personal social media to post about market trends. This is:

A. Unethical and prohibited
B. Acceptable if pre-approved by the firm and monitored
C. Permitted without restriction
D. Never allowed under any circumstances

Question 50

An IAR's annual ADV update must be filed:

A. Within 60 days of fiscal year-end
B. Annually within 90 days of fiscal year-end
C. Only when fees change
D. Monthly

Question 51

Which of the following must an investment adviser disclose to clients?

A. The name of every portfolio manager they've ever hired
B. Any material disciplinary action within the last 10 years
C. Every trade executed in the last quarter
D. The salaries of firm executives

Question 52

A client files a complaint with the Administrator. The Administrator may:

A. Order restitution before a hearing
B. Require testimony, documents, and issue subpoenas
C. Immediately freeze the adviser's assets
D. Refer the case to FINRA for enforcement

Question 53

A broker-dealer sells securities to a client and fails to disclose a 2% markup. This is:

A. Acceptable for small transactions
B. Prohibited and may result in a civil liability
C. Permissible if the client is an institution
D. Unethical, but not illegal

Question 54

An agent wishes to moonlight as a tax preparer. This is allowed if:

A. The firm approves and it's disclosed if there's a conflict

B. The client signs a release form
C. The IRS provides a license
D. No disclosure is necessary

Question 55

Which of the following actions would be considered fraud under the USA?

A. Charging higher commissions to new clients
B. Omitting a material fact from a sale
C. Offering limited partnerships only to qualified investors
D. Recommending a risky security

Question 56

An agent is suspended in one state. What effect does this have in another state?

A. None

B. The Administrator in the second state may take similar action

C. The suspension only applies to exempt securities

D. The agent can still work with institutions

Question 57

Which of the following individuals is considered a "person" under the Uniform Securities Act?

A. A minor

B. A deceased individual

C. A legal partnership

D. An agent under supervision

Question 58

An adviser takes custody of client assets but fails to notify the Administrator. This is:

A. A disclosure error but not a violation

B. Permitted if the adviser is federally covered

C. A violation of the USA

D. Allowed if the client approves in writing

Question 59

An IAR recommends an unsuitable investment that results in a loss. The client:

A. Has no recourse if a prospectus was delivered

B. May file a civil suit for damages

C. May only complain to the SEC
D. Must accept market risk

Question 60
Under the USA, which of the following is **not** a defined security?

A. Equipment leasing certificate
B. Voting trust certificate
C. Fixed annuity
D. Preorganization certificate

Question 61
A Canadian broker-dealer with no office in the U.S. is exempt from registration if:

A. They deal only with retail U.S. clients
B. They deal only with institutional U.S. clients
C. They're approved by the SEC
D. They register in one U.S. state

Question 62
A new IAR fails to disclose a past personal bankruptcy. This is:

A. Prohibited if the bankruptcy was within 10 years
B. Acceptable if unrelated to securities
C. Only an issue if it involved fraud
D. Always cause for automatic denial of registration

Question 63
The term "offer to sell" under the USA includes:

A. A gift of an assessable security
B. A gift of non-assessable securities

C. Delivery of a final prospectus only
D. Verbal recommendations

Question 64

Which of the following statements is true about registration by coordination?

A. It applies only to securities listed on an exchange
B. It is a federal-only process
C. It coordinates state registration with SEC filings
D. It requires all states to approve simultaneously

Question 65

An Administrator may deny, revoke, or suspend a registration if the applicant:

A. Fails to meet performance targets
B. Is convicted of any felony in the past 10 years
C. Loses money in a client's account
D. Has over 10 client complaints

SIMULATED SERIES 63 EXAM – ANSWER KEY & EXPLANATIONS

(QUESTIONS 1–65)

PASSING SCORE: 43/60 SCORED QUESTIONS (72%)

1. C – Agents must register in any state where they sell to retail clients.
2. B – Commodities and futures contracts (not the underlying securities) are not considered securities under the USA.
3. B – IARs must register when they provide personalized advice to clients in a state.
4. C – Charging disclosed commissions is ethical and legal.

5. C – Administrators may issue subpoenas, but criminal penalties require judicial action.
6. D – All listed are federally covered securities, so the answer is all of the above.
7. B – A consent to service of process allows the Administrator to act as legal representative in lawsuits.
8. B – State Administrators can enforce cease and desist orders for violations in their state.
9. B – Foreign governments (like Canada) issuing securities are generally exempt.
10. B – Firms may hold mail temporarily with written client instruction, typically up to 3 months.
11. C – Recommending suitable investments is expected.
12. A – Private placements are exempt if sold to 35 or fewer non-institutional clients.
13. A – Clerical staff who don't solicit or execute trades aren't agents.
14. B – A broker-dealer without an office transacting with institutions only is exempt.
15. C – Both the firm and the customer must give written consent to profit sharing.
16. B – The firm must notify the Administrator when an IAR changes states.
17. B – Surety bonds protect clients against adviser fraud or misconduct.
18. C – The trade is legal if the security is exempt or federally covered.
19. B – A felony conviction within 10 years is grounds for denial.
20. A – Clients may rescind the sale and seek restitution.
21. C – Agents must mark the account as deceased and await instructions.
22. D – Agents may not borrow from clients unless they're banks or family.
23. C – Exemptions can be revoked with notice and opportunity for a hearing.
24. D – Advisers need not disclose receptionist background.

25. A – Saying "I've invested, so it will work" implies a guarantee, which is prohibited.
26. C – Advisers with custody must notify, be audited annually, and meet net worth rules.
27. B – Social media is not a required brochure item.
28. B – Civil suits under the USA: 2 years from discovery or 3 years from violation.
29. C – Variable annuities are securities and require registration.
30. A – Administrators may require a surety bond for custody or discretion.
31. B – Selling non-exempt, unregistered securities is prohibited unless an exemption applies.
32. B – A newsletter with specific recommendations must be filed.
33. C – Omitting material facts is unethical.
34. B – Advertising guarantees is prohibited.
35. C – Administrators may issue cease and desist orders without prior hearings.
36. C – Soft dollar arrangements must benefit clients, not the adviser.
37. B – Discretion requires written client authorization.
38. C – Advisers with $110M+ AUM must register federally.
39. C – Registration becomes effective 30 days after filing unless denied or delayed.
40. C – Testimonials are allowed if they follow SEC marketing rules and proper disclosures.
41. C – The Administrator may act without prior hearing if public interest is at risk.
42. C – A joint account requires written agreement from both parties.
43. B – U.S. government securities are exempt.
44. C – Blanket recommendations violate fiduciary duty.
45. C – A receptionist leaving is not a material change.
46. B – Civil liability includes original investment + interest + court costs + attorney's fees.

47. A – Agents must notify their firm in writing and receive approval before private deals.
48. A – Failure to pay registration fees can result in denial.
49. B – Firm-monitored social media use is allowed with compliance controls.
50. B – ADV updates are filed within 90 days of the adviser's fiscal year-end.
51. B – Advisers must disclose material disciplinary history within the past 10 years.
52. B – Administrators can issue subpoenas and request documentation.
53. B – Failing to disclose a markup is a USA violation and civil liability.
54. A – Outside business activities like tax prep must be approved and disclosed.
55. B – Omitting material facts is considered fraud.
56. B – Other states may take similar actions based on reciprocal agreements.
57. C – A partnership is a person; minors and deceased individuals are not.
58. C – Taking custody without notifying the Administrator is a violation.
59. B – Clients can sue for damages if the recommendation was unsuitable.
60. C – Fixed annuities are not securities; all others listed are.
61. B – Canadian BDs may be exempt if working only with U.S. institutions.
62. A – Bankruptcies within 10 years must be disclosed.
63. A – A gift of assessable stock is treated as a sale/offer.
64. C – Coordination links state registration to SEC filings.
65. B – Any felony within the last 10 years is grounds for denial.

CHAPTER 15
ANSWER KEYS AND RATIONALES

Part I: Series 6 – Practice Questions 1–20
Each entry includes:
Correct Answer
Explanation
Why the other options are incorrect

Question 1
Which of the following products is NOT sold by someone holding only a Series 6 license?

Correct Answer: C. Individual stocks

A Series 6 license allows the sale of packaged securities like mutual funds and variable products. It does **not** allow for the sale of individual stocks or bonds.

Not Correct Answer(s):

A: Mutual funds are permitted under Series 6.
B: Variable annuities are also included.
D: Unit Investment Trusts (UITs) are permitted products.

Question 2
Which of the following is a characteristic of a mutual fund?

Correct Answer: A. It is a redeemable security

Mutual funds are redeemable, meaning investors sell shares back to the fund, not on a secondary market.

Not Correct Answer(s):

B: Closed-end funds trade on exchanges; mutual funds do not.
C: Mutual funds must calculate NAV at least once per business day.
D: They are bought and sold at NAV + sales charge, not prices fluctuating throughout the day.

Question 3
Which document must be delivered at or prior to the solicitation of a mutual fund?

Correct Answer: A. Prospectus

The SEC requires that a statutory prospectus be delivered before or at the time of solicitation for mutual funds.

Not Correct Answer(s):
B-D: Statements and confirmations come after purchase, not before solicitation.

Question 4
What is the primary purpose of a breakpoint in mutual fund sales?

Correct Answer: D. To offer discounts based on the size of the investment

Breakpoints are volume discounts designed to reduce the sales charge for large mutual fund investments.

Not Correct Answer(s):

A: Breakpoints are not for cost recovery.
B: They do not prevent frequent trading.
C: They aren't imposed as penalties.

Question 5
Which of the following securities can be sold by a Series 6 representative?

Correct Answer: B. Variable universal life insurance

Series 6 reps can sell variable insurance products, mutual funds, and UITs. Individual securities are outside their scope.

Not Correct Answer(s):

A/C/D: These involve individual equity/bond transactions, which require a Series 7 license.

Question 6
Which type of investment company issues shares that are bought and sold in the secondary market?

Correct Answer: C. Closed-end fund
Closed-end funds are traded on secondary markets like stocks.

Not Correct Answer(s):

A/B/D: Open-end funds (mutual funds), UITs, and variable annuities are not traded on exchanges.

Question 7
Which term refers to the total annual expenses of a mutual fund expressed as a percentage of average net assets?

Correct Answer: A. Expense ratio

The expense ratio helps investors compare cost efficiency between funds.

Not Correct Answer(s):
B: Load is a sales charge.
C: NAV is the per-share value of fund assets.
D: Turnover rate reflects trading frequency, not expenses.

Question 8
What is the maximum front-end sales load allowed under FINRA rules for mutual funds?

Correct Answer: C. 8.5%
FINRA caps mutual fund sales loads at **8.5%** of the offering price.

Not Correct Answer(s):

A/B: Too low
D: Too high

Question 9
What is the NAV per share if a mutual fund has $100 million in assets, $5 million in liabilities, and 10 million shares outstanding?

Correct Answer: A. $9.50

NAV = (Assets – Liabilities) ÷ Shares Outstanding
= ($100M - $5M) ÷ 10M = $95M ÷ 10M = **$9.50**

Question 10
Which of the following would reduce the NAV of a mutual fund?

Correct Answer: D. A dividend payment

When dividends are paid out, NAV drops by the amount of the distribution.

Not Correct Answer(s):

A/B/C: Market gains and income received increase NAV or leave it unchanged.

Question 11
Which of the following is true of Class B shares?

Correct Answer: C. They convert to Class A shares after a holding period

Class B shares carry a back-end sales charge and convert to Class A over time, which may reduce expenses.

Not Correct Answer(s):

A: B shares don't charge a front-end load.
B: There is a sales charge, but it's deferred.
D: Ongoing expenses are often higher for B shares.

Question 12
The term "breakpoint sale" refers to:

Correct Answer: B. An unethical practice of keeping a customer's investment below a discount level

Reps must not purposely split client purchases to avoid giving them a discount—this violates FINRA rules.

Not Correct Answer(s):

A: A legitimate large investment is not a breakpoint sale.
C/D: Misleading terms

Question 13
An investor using a letter of intent (LOI) must invest the required amount within:

Correct Answer: C. 13 months

LOIs give investors 13 months to reach a breakpoint level and receive an immediate discount.

Not Correct Answer(s):

A/B/D: Incorrect time frames.

Question 14
Which fund structure pays commissions to brokers at the time of sale?

Correct Answer: A. Class A shares

Class A shares carry upfront sales charges, which compensate the broker immediately.

Not Correct Answer(s):

B: B shares use back-end loads.
C: C shares have level loads.
D: No-load funds don't pay commissions.

Question 15
Which investment company structure is typically not actively managed?

Correct Answer: C. Unit Investment Trust (UIT)
UITs buy a fixed portfolio and do not have active managers.

Not Correct Answer(s):
A/B/D: These involve professional portfolio management.

Question 16
Which of the following can reduce a client's mutual fund sales charges?

Correct Answer: A. Rights of accumulation

Rights of accumulation allow investors to count prior investments to earn breakpoints.

Not Correct Answer(s):

B/C: Not related to discounts
D: Share classes do not reduce charges retroactively

Question 17
Who manages a mutual fund portfolio?

Correct Answer: B. Investment adviser
The investment adviser is responsible for day-to-day portfolio decisions.

Not Correct Answer(s):
A/C/D: Board oversees the adviser but doesn't manage investments.

Question 18
What happens when a mutual fund distributes capital gains?

Correct Answer: A. Investors are taxed whether they receive the gains or reinvest them

Capital gains are taxable income in the year distributed, regardless of reinvestment.

Not Correct Answer(s):

B/C: No tax avoidance
D: Not tax-deferred

Question 19
Which of the following is NOT a redeemable security?

Correct Answer: B. Closed-end fund
Closed-end funds trade on exchanges and are not redeemable.

Not Correct Answer(s):
A/C/D: Mutual funds, variable annuities, and UITs are redeemable.

Question 20
The NAV of a mutual fund increases when:

Correct Answer: A. The value of the underlying securities increases
NAV reflects net assets, so when portfolio value increases, NAV rises.

Not Correct Answer(s):
B-D: These do not impact NAV positively.

Question 21
What does a mutual fund's Statement of Additional Information (SAI) provide?

Correct Answer: D. More detailed information than the prospectus

The SAI supplements the prospectus with in-depth operational, legal, and financial details, but isn't required to be delivered unless requested.

Not Correct Answer(s):
A/B/C: These are all covered briefly in the main prospectus.

Question 22
Which of the following best describes dollar-cost averaging?

Correct Answer: B. Investing a fixed dollar amount at regular intervals

Dollar-cost averaging helps smooth out the impact of market **volatility** over time by buying more shares when prices are low.

Not Correct Answer(s):

A: You do buy more shares at lower prices, but that's not the definition.
C: It doesn't eliminate risk.
D: It's not used for timing markets.

Question 23
Which mutual fund share class typically has the highest 12b-1 fees?

Correct Answer: C. Class C shares

Class C shares carry level loads and higher ongoing 12b-1 fees, making them expensive long-term.

Not Correct Answer(s):

A/B: Class A and B typically have lower ongoing fees.
D: No-load funds do not have 12b-1 fees.

Question 24
What is the primary regulatory document that governs mutual fund advertising?

Correct Answer: B. SEC Rule 482
SEC Rule 482 governs advertisements for mutual funds, including performance disclosures and content restrictions.

Not Correct Answer(s):
A: FINRA Rule 2210 governs communications broadly, not specifically mutual fund ads.

C/D: Not applicable here.

Question 25
A letter of intent is valid for how long?

Correct Answer: A. 13 months
Letters of intent (LOI) allow clients to receive breakpoints immediately, as long as the total investment is made within 13 months.

Not Correct Answer(s):
B/C/D: Incorrect timeframes.

Question 26
What does the term "front-end load" refer to?

Correct Answer: D. A sales charge paid when buying shares

A front-end load is an upfront commission taken from the investor's initial investment.

Not Correct Answer(s):
A/B/C: These refer to ongoing or deferred charges.

Question 27
Which type of mutual fund share class is most appropriate for a long-term investor making a large investment?

Correct Answer: A. Class A shares

Class A shares provide breakpoints on large investments and have lower ongoing expenses—ideal for long-term investors.

Not Correct Answer(s):

B: B shares have higher expenses and deferred sales charges.
C: C shares are better for short-term.
D: No-load funds are possible but don't offer breakpoint discounts.

Question 28
Which of the following is TRUE about mutual fund taxation?

Correct Answer: C. Capital gains and dividends are taxable in the year distributed

Whether reinvested or not, all distributions are taxable in the year received.

Not Correct Answer(s):
A/B/D: These misstate the tax treatment of mutual fund distributions.

Question 29
Which of the following is a characteristic of an open-end investment company?

Correct Answer: A. Issues redeemable shares
Mutual funds (open-end companies) issue redeemable shares, not traded on secondary markets.

Not Correct Answer(s):

B: Secondary trading applies to closed-end funds.
C: NAV is calculated once daily.
D: No limit on shares issued.

Question 30
When must a mutual fund compute its NAV?

Correct Answer: D. At least once per business day
By law, funds must compute their NAV daily, usually at market close.

Not Correct Answer(s):
A-C: Too frequent or not required.

Question 31
An investor pays $10.50 per share for a mutual fund with an NAV of $10. What is the sales charge?

Correct Answer: C. 4.76%
Sales Charge = (POP - NAV) ÷ POP
= (10.50 - 10) ÷ 10.50 = 0.50 ÷ 10.50 = **4.76%**

Question 32
Which of the following is required in a mutual fund prospectus?

Correct Answer: B. Investment objectives and risks
A prospectus must disclose objectives, risks, expenses, and performance.

Not Correct Answer(s):

A: Not required
C: Custodian identity is not mandatory
D: Sales commissions are disclosed but not highlighted as a "requirement"

Question 33
A mutual fund that reinvests dividends and capital gains into new shares will:

Correct Answer: D. Still trigger a taxable event for the shareholder

Even reinvested distributions are taxable in the year received.

Not Correct Answer(s):
A/B: No tax deferral
C: Not true unless in tax-advantaged account

Question 34
Which of the following investments is considered redeemable?

Correct Answer: B. Mutual fund shares

Only mutual funds, UITs, and variable annuities are redeemable. Closed-end funds are not.

Not Correct Answer(s):
A/C/D: Not redeemable securities.

Question 35
Which mutual fund share class typically has a contingent deferred sales charge?

Correct Answer: B. Class B shares
Class B shares charge a CDSC that decreases over time.

Not Correct Answer(s):
A: Class A has front-end loads.
C: C shares have level loads.
D: No-load funds don't charge CDSCs.

Question 36
NAV is affected by which of the following?

Correct Answer: C. Market value of underlying portfolio securities
NAV = (Assets - Liabilities) / Shares Outstanding → driven by portfolio values.

Not Correct Answer(s):
A/B/D: These don't directly change NAV.

Question 37
Which of the following charges covers marketing and distribution of mutual funds?

Correct Answer: A. 12b-1 fees
12b-1 fees pay for advertising, promotional expenses, and sometimes commissions.

Not Correct Answer(s):
B: Management fee covers investment advisory
C: CDSC is sales-related
D: Operating expenses cover general costs

Question 38
When purchasing mutual fund shares, which price does the investor pay?

Correct Answer: B. Public offering price
The POP = NAV + sales charge → what the investor pays.

Not Correct Answer(s):

A: NAV is for redemptions
C/D: These aren't pricing models

Question 39
Which of the following statements about mutual fund sales literature is TRUE?

Correct Answer: D. It must be preceded or accompanied by a prospectus

FINRA and SEC require sales literature be preceded or accompanied by a current prospectus.

Not Correct Answer(s):
A/B/C: These are either incomplete or inaccurate.

Question 40
A fund has an NAV of $20 and a sales charge of 5%. What is the POP?

Correct Answer: C. $21.05
POP = NAV ÷ (100% - Sales Charge %)
= 20 ÷ (1 - 0.05) = 20 ÷ 0.95 = **$21.05**

Question 41
Which of the following terms refers to the dollar amount that an investor must invest to receive a reduced sales charge in a mutual fund?

Correct Answer: A. Breakpoint
A breakpoint is a sales charge discount based on the amount invested in mutual funds.

Not Correct Answer(s):
B: Rights of accumulation refer to previous investments counting toward breakpoints.
C: NAV is the price per share.
D: POP is what the investor pays.

Question 42
Which of the following statements about mutual fund taxation is TRUE?

Correct Answer: B. Reinvested dividends are taxable in the year received

Whether received in cash or reinvested, dividends are taxed in the year distributed.

Not Correct Answer(s):
A: Capital gains are taxed even if reinvested.
C: Only qualified dividends receive preferential tax treatment.
D: Distributions are never tax-free unless in retirement accounts.

Question 43
Which of the following fees is disclosed in a mutual fund's expense ratio?

Correct Answer: D. Investment advisory fees
The expense ratio includes management (advisory) fees, administrative fees, and 12b-1 fees.

Not Correct Answer(s):
A/B: Front- and back-end loads are not part of the expense ratio.
C: CDSCs are contingent charges, not annual expenses.

Question 44
An investor wants to invest $48,000 in a mutual fund with a breakpoint at $50,000. Which option helps them reach the breakpoint?

Correct Answer: C. Signing a letter of intent

A letter of intent (LOI) allows the investor to receive the breakpoint discount upfront if they commit to investing enough over 13 months.

Not Correct Answer(s):

A: Rights of accumulation apply to past investments.
B: Class A shares don't automatically reduce the load.
D: Averaging does not affect loads.

Question 45
Which of the following would decrease a fund's NAV per share?

Correct Answer: A. Dividend distribution

Not Correct Answer(s):

Paying a dividend reduces the fund's assets, lowering NAV.
B/C/D: Unrealized gains or appreciation increase or leave NAV unaffected.

Question 46
What does the term "no-load" mean in mutual fund investing?

Correct Answer: D. The fund charges no front-end or back-end sales load

A no-load fund has no sales charge, though it may still have management fees or 12b-1 fees (up to 0.25%).

Not Correct Answer(s):

A: All funds have some expenses.
B/C: There's no such thing as "free" trading or NAV-purchase guarantees.

Question 47
Which of the following best describes the term "NAV"?

Correct Answer: A. Value of assets minus liabilities, divided by shares outstanding

NAV = (Total Assets - Liabilities) / Outstanding Shares

Not Correct Answer(s):

B: That's the definition of POP with a load.
C/D: Misinterpret the calculation.

Question 48
If a mutual fund has $80 million in assets, $5 million in liabilities, and 10 million shares outstanding, what is the NAV?

Correct Answer: B. $7.50
NAV = ($80M - $5M) ÷ 10M = **$7.50**

Question 49
Which of the following is TRUE regarding mutual fund prospectus delivery?

Correct Answer: C. It must be delivered at or before the time of sale

SEC rules require that the **statutory prospectus** be delivered before or at the time of sale.

Not Correct Answer(s):
A: Not after
B: Summary is acceptable only under specific conditions
D: Brochures are not substitutes for the prospectus

Question 50
Who is responsible for safeguarding the mutual fund's assets?

Correct Answer: D. The custodian

The custodian bank holds fund assets in trust to prevent fraud or loss.

Not Correct Answer(s):

A: Adviser manages the portfolio.
B: Transfer agent handles recordkeeping.
C: Sponsor distributes shares.

Question 51
Which of the following may be considered a "front-end load"?

Correct Answer: C. Sales charge deducted from an investor's initial investment

A front-end load is taken off the top of the investment, reducing the amount going into the fund.

Not Correct Answer(s):
A/B: These are different costs
D: NAV is not a load

Question 52
The 12b-1 fee is used for what purpose?
Correct Answer: A. To pay for marketing and distribution expenses

12b-1 fees cover advertising, sales literature, and compensation to brokers.

Not Correct Answer(s):
B: Advisory fees are separate
C: Custody fees are operational
D: Taxes are not paid via 12b-1

Question 53
When is the POP equal to the NAV in mutual fund purchases?

Correct Answer: B. When the fund does not charge a sales load
In no-load funds, NAV = POP since no sales charge is added.

Not Correct Answer(s):

A/C/D: These all describe loaded funds or incorrect pricing logic.

Question 54
Which of the following is an investment company under the Investment Company Act of 1940?

Correct Answer: A. Mutual fund

A mutual fund is an open-end investment company regulated under the 1940 Act.

Not Correct Answer(s):

B: REITs are not investment companies.

C: Banks are not included.

D: Insurance companies are regulated separately.

Question 55

Which party ensures mutual fund shares are properly issued and redeemed?

Correct Answer: B. Transfer agent

The transfer agent keeps investor records, issues and cancels shares, and handles distributions.

Not Correct Answer(s):

A: Custodian holds the assets

C: Adviser manages investments

D: Underwriter handles sales

Question 56

Which of the following is TRUE about mutual fund investment objectives?

Correct Answer: C. They are stated in the prospectus

All funds must disclose their objectives (growth, income, etc.) in the prospectus.

Not Correct Answer(s):

A/B/D: These misrepresent how objectives are handled.

Question 57
Which of the following is considered a regulated investment company under Subchapter M?

Correct Answer: A. A mutual fund that distributes 90% of income

To avoid taxation at the corporate level, funds must distribute at least 90% of net income.

Not Correct Answer(s):
B/C/D: These are unrelated or misstate the rule.

Question 58
Which of the following is FALSE regarding mutual fund distributions?

Correct Answer: C. Reinvested capital gains are tax-deferred

FALSE: Reinvested capital gains are taxable in the year received, not deferred.

Not Correct Answer(s):
A/B/D: These are all true.

Question 59
An investor is concerned with minimizing tax liability. Which feature of mutual funds may help?

Correct Answer: D. Tax-efficient management strategies

Funds using tax-loss harvesting or low turnover strategies may help reduce taxes.

Not Correct Answer(s):

A: Frequent trading increases taxes
B: 12b-1 fees are costs
C: Reinvestment does not avoid taxes

Question 60
What is a contingent deferred sales charge (CDSC)?

Correct Answer: B. A fee charged when selling fund shares before a certain period

CDSC (back-end load) is imposed when investors redeem shares early, common with Class B shares.

Not Correct Answer(s):
A/C/D: Mislabel or describe different charges.

Question 61
What does the transfer agent NOT do for a mutual fund?

Correct Answer: C. Manage the fund's portfolio
The transfer agent is responsible for maintaining records of share ownership, processing purchase and redemption requests, and distributing dividends.

Not Correct Answer(s):

A. Maintain shareholder records – This is a core responsibility of the transfer agent.
B. Issue and cancel shares – Also performed by the transfer agent.
D. Distribute dividends – Transfer agents distribute dividends and capital gains to investors.

Question 62
Which of the following is TRUE about a mutual fund's board of directors?

Correct Answer: D. At least 40% must be independent

The Investment Company Act of 1940 mandates that at least 40% of board members must be independent.

Not Correct Answer(s):
A. All members must be employees – False; many are independent.
B. The board determines daily NAV – NAV is calculated by the fund accountant, not the board.
C. They choose fund investments – The fund manager or investment adviser handles this.

Question 63
Which fee is NOT included in a mutual fund's expense ratio?

Correct Answer: C. Sales load

Sales loads (front-end, back-end) are transaction-based and not included in the annual operating expense ratio.

Not Correct Answer(s):

A. 12b-1 fees – Included in the expense ratio.
B. Management fees – Also included.
D. Administrative fees – Included as part of fund operations.

Question 64
What is the benefit of reinvesting mutual fund dividends?

Correct Answer: A. Compounding growth over time

Reinvesting dividends allows you to earn returns on reinvested income, leading to compounding growth.

Not Correct Answer(s):

B. It avoids taxation – Incorrect; reinvested dividends are still taxable.
C. It provides guaranteed gains – There are no guarantees in investing.
D. It prevents NAV from declining – Dividends reduce NAV when paid.

Question 65
A mutual fund switches from quarterly to monthly dividend distributions. What is the tax consequence?

Correct Answer: D. All dividends are still taxable in the year received

Frequency of dividends doesn't affect taxability.

Not Correct Answer(s):

A. Monthly dividends are tax-free – Incorrect.
B. Only qualified dividends are taxed – Not accurate; non-qualified ones are taxed too.
C. Reinvested dividends are tax-deferred – No, they're still taxed.

Question 66
Who regulates the content of mutual fund advertisements?

Correct Answer: C. SEC and FINRA

The SEC (federal) and FINRA (SRO) jointly regulate fund advertising for compliance and transparency.

Not Correct Answer(s):

A. SIPC – Provides insurance, not advertising regulation.

B. IRS – Handles taxes, not advertising.

D. State regulators – Primarily enforce state laws, not national advertising standards.

Question 67

What happens to the NAV when a fund pays a dividend?

Correct Answer: A. It decreases by the dividend amount

Paying dividends reduces the fund's assets, which lowers NAV.

Not Correct Answer(s):

B. It increases by the dividend amount – False.

C. NAV stays the same – No, it drops.

D. NAV is recalculated weekly – It is recalculated daily.

Question 68

The purpose of a breakpoint schedule is to:

Correct Answer: B. Reduce the sales charge as the investment increases

Breakpoints provide discounts on front-end loads when investing large amounts in Class A shares.

Not Correct Answer(s):

A. Increase NAV for large investors – NAV doesn't change based on who buys.

C. Offer different share classes – Share classes are separate from breakpoints.

D. Defer taxes on gains – Not related.

Question 69

Which of the following actions would be considered a breakpoint sale violation?

Correct Answer: A. Splitting a customer's purchase to avoid giving a discount

This deprives the investor of a rightful discount and is unethical.

Not Correct Answer(s):

B. Recommending Class B shares – Not a violation on its own.
C. Reinvesting dividends – Encouraged, not a violation.
D. Offering a letter of intent – Legitimate tool for breakpoint eligibility.

Question 70
The maximum 12b-1 fee for a fund to still be labeled "no-load" is:

Correct Answer: C. 0.25%

According to FINRA rules, a fund with a 12b-1 fee higher than 0.25% cannot be labeled "no-load."

Not Correct Answer(s):

A. 1% – That's the maximum 12b-1 fee overall, not for no-load status.
B. 0.75% – Too high for a no-load fund.
D. 0% – No-load funds can have fees up to 0.25%.

Question 71
What is the consequence of failing to meet the terms of a letter of intent (LOI)?

Correct Answer: D. The investor must pay the full applicable sales charge

The fund will retroactively apply the correct, higher sales charge.

Not Correct Answer(s):

A. The investor receives a refund – No refund is granted.
B. The LOI is automatically extended – Extensions are not automatic.
C. The shares are forfeited – No, the investor still owns them.

Question 72
Which of the following is TRUE regarding the investment adviser to a mutual fund?

Correct Answer: B. It is paid a fee based on assets under management

Advisers earn a percentage of AUM—this aligns the adviser's interests with fund growth.

Not Correct Answer(s):

A. It is paid based on performance only – That's more typical of hedge funds.
C. It holds custody of fund assets – That's the custodian's role.
D. It distributes fund shares – That's the underwriter's job.

Question 73
The primary difference between open-end and closed-end companies is:

Correct Answer: C. Open-end funds are redeemable, closed-end are not

Open-end funds allow shares to be redeemed at NAV; closed-end funds trade on the secondary market.

Not Correct Answer(s):

A. Closed-end funds charge loads – Not always.

B. Open-end funds are ETFs – Incorrect; ETFs are separate structures.
D. Closed-end funds reinvest dividends – Both types can do this.

Question 74
Which term applies when fund shares are sold back to the issuer?

Correct Answer: B. Redemption
Mutual fund shares are redeemable directly through the fund.

Not Correct Answer(s):

A. Withdrawal – Too vague.
C. Liquidation – Refers to winding up a fund.
D. Transfer – Refers to ownership changes, not sales.

Question 75
What is the difference between NAV and POP?

Correct Answer: A. POP includes the sales load

POP = NAV + front-end sales charge.

Not Correct Answer(s):

B. NAV includes commissions – No, NAV is net of fund assets.
C. POP is the market price – Incorrect; mutual funds don't trade on the market.
D. NAV equals POP – Only in no-load funds.

Question 76
A mutual fund investor pays $10.60 per share. NAV is $10. What is the sales charge %?

Correct Answer: C. 5.66%

(10.60 - 10) ÷ 10.60 = 0.0566 = **5.66%**

Not Correct Answer(s):

A/B/D – These are incorrect calculations.

Question 77

What is the purpose of the fund custodian?

Correct Answer: D. Safeguard the fund's assets

The custodian ensures that fund assets are secure and properly accounted for.

Not Correct Answer(s):

A. Distribute fund shares – That's the underwriter.

B. Manage client portfolios – The adviser does that.

C. Register fund investors – That's the transfer agent.

Question 78

A fund that maintains a fixed portfolio of securities is known as a:

Correct Answer: C. Unit Investment Trust

UITs have a static portfolio and are passively managed.

Not Correct Answer(s):

A. Mutual fund – Actively managed.

B. Closed-end fund – Traded and often actively managed.

D. ETF – Actively or passively managed but not fixed.

Question 79

Which of the following statements is TRUE about UITs?

Correct Answer: B. They do not have portfolio managers

UITs are unmanaged once the portfolio is established.

Not Correct Answer(s):
A. They trade on secondary markets – They don't.
C. They charge high 12b-1 fees – Typically low fees.
D. They offer active management – False.

Question 80
The public offering price of a mutual fund is determined by:

Correct Answer: D. NAV plus the applicable sales charge
This is the formula for POP for Class A shares.

Not Correct Answer(s):

A. Market demand – Not relevant for mutual funds.
B. Net investment income – Affects distributions, not POP.
C. Board decision – POP is formula-driven, not set arbitrarily.

Question 81
Which of the following transactions is considered a violation of FINRA rules?

Correct Answer: A. Selling mutual fund shares just before dividends are paid (selling dividends)

"Selling dividends" is unethical because it misleads investors into thinking they are gaining extra value.

Not Correct Answer(s):

B. Reinvesting dividends – Perfectly acceptable and encouraged.

C. Switching from Class B to Class A shares – Not a violation if justified.
D. Purchasing shares with a letter of intent – Legitimate practice.

Question 82
What must be provided to a prospective mutual fund investor at the time of sale?

Correct Answer: C. Prospectus
A fund's statutory prospectus must be delivered before or at the time of sale.

A. Fund fact sheet – Not required and doesn't satisfy regulatory obligation.
B. Summary prospectus only – Only acceptable if certain SEC conditions are met.
D. Statement of additional information – Must be available upon request, not mandatory upfront.

Not Correct Answer(s):

Question 83
A mutual fund manager who actively buys and sells securities may generate:

Correct Answer: B. Higher capital gains distributions

Active trading can lead to short-term capital gains, increasing taxable distributions to shareholders.

A. Reduced turnover – Active management increases turnover.
C. Fewer taxable events – More trades = more tax events.
D. Lower expense ratios – Trading increases expenses.

Question 84
Class C shares are most suitable for investors with:

Correct Answer: B. A short-term investment horizon
C shares have level loads and are good for short- to mid-term holdings due to lower upfront charges.

Not Correct Answer(s):

A. Long-term goals – Class A shares are more cost-effective over time.
C. Large investments – A shares offer breakpoints.
D. No need for liquidity – Doesn't relate to share class suitability.

Question 85
Which of the following is an advantage of Class A shares?

Correct Answer: C. Lower ongoing expenses

Not Correct Answer(s):
A shares typically have lower 12b-1 fees than B or C shares.

A. No front-end load – Incorrect; A shares *do* have front-end loads.
B. Highest breakpoints – All A share investors can qualify for breakpoints; it's not about high or low.
D. No fees at redemption – Not the defining feature; B shares have CDSCs.

Question 86
What is the role of the principal underwriter of a mutual fund?

Correct Answer: A. Distribute the fund's shares to dealers and investors

Also called the fund sponsor, this party sells fund shares through dealers or directly.

Not Correct Answer(s):

B. Provide investment advice – That's the adviser's job.
C. Maintain shareholder records – Transfer agent's role.
D. Safeguard fund assets – Custodian's responsibility.

Question 87
Which type of mutual fund share typically converts into Class A shares after a certain period?

Correct Answer: B. Class B shares

Not Correct Answer(s):

B shares often **convert to A shares** after 6-8 years, eliminating higher 12b-1 fees.

A. Class A shares – No conversion occurs.
C. Class C shares – Do not convert.
D. No-load shares – Not applicable.

Question 88
Which of the following is true about a back-end sales load?

Correct Answer: D. It decreases the longer the investor holds the shares

Back-end loads (CDSCs) decline over time and may disappear after 5–7 years.

Not Correct Answer(s):

A. It's charged at purchase – That's a front-end load.
B. It's deducted annually – Incorrect.
C. It increases over time – False; it declines.

Question 89
A mutual fund's turnover ratio indicates:

Correct Answer: A. The frequency with which portfolio holdings are bought and sold

High turnover = active management and possibly more taxable events.

Not Correct Answer(s):

B. Fund's dividend yield – Not related.
C. How often shares are issued – Irrelevant.
D. NAV fluctuations – Unrelated to turnover.

Question 90
An investor wants automatic reinvestment of fund distributions. What must be disclosed?

Correct Answer: C. Distributions are still taxable even if reinvested

Not Correct Answer(s):

The IRS taxes dividends and gains regardless of whether they're reinvested.
A. Reinvested shares are tax-deferred – Incorrect.
B. Reinvestment avoids capital gains tax – It doesn't.
D. IRS waives tax for reinvestment – False.

Question 91
Which disclosure is required in mutual fund advertising that includes performance data?

Correct Answer: D. Past performance does not guarantee future results

This SEC-mandated disclaimer must be present in performance marketing.

Not Correct Answer(s):

- **A. No investment losses are possible** – False.
- **B. Dividends are guaranteed** – Never guaranteed.
- **C. The fund is risk-free** – Misleading and untrue.

Question 92
Which party calculates the NAV of a mutual fund?

Correct Answer: B. The fund's accountant or pricing service
NAV is computed daily using the total assets – liabilities ÷ shares outstanding.

Not Correct Answer(s):

- **A. Transfer agent** – Not responsible.
- **C. Investment adviser** – Oversees investments, not NAV.
- **D. Custodian** – Holds assets, doesn't calculate NAV.

Question 93
What is the tax implication of a mutual fund capital gains distribution?

Correct Answer: A. Taxed in the year distributed, even if reinvested
Reinvestment doesn't defer or eliminate tax obligations.

B. Tax-deferred until shares are sold – False.
C. Only taxed when taken in cash – Incorrect.
D. Tax-free in all accounts – Only if in a tax-advantaged account like an IRA.

Not Correct Answer(s):

Question 94
A fund advertises a 5% yield. What must be true?

Correct Answer: C. The figure must reflect actual income distributions

Not Correct Answer(s):
The SEC requires yield data to be based on actual results, not projections.

A. It can be based on projections – Not allowed.
B. It includes capital gains – Yield excludes capital gains.
D. It is not subject to regulation – It definitely is.

Question 95
When can a mutual fund accept a purchase order?

Correct Answer: A. When the fund receives a completed application and payment

Both are required to open and fund the account.

Not Correct Answer(s):

B. When the application is signed – Payment is also needed.
C. After a verbal agreement – Not sufficient.
D. Once the investor gets the prospectus – That's just disclosure, not execution.

Question 96
Which fund is least likely to distribute capital gains?

Correct Answer: D. Index fund

Passive index funds trade infrequently, generating fewer taxable events.

Not Correct Answer(s):

A. Growth fund – Active trading = more capital gains.
B. Sector fund – Typically actively managed.
C. Small-cap fund – Higher turnover often.

Question 97
A prospectus must be updated at least:

Correct Answer: B. Every 12 months
SEC requires funds to file an updated prospectus annually.

Not Correct Answer(s):

A. Every 6 months – Too frequent.
C. Every 24 months – Too long.
D. Only after material changes – Updates are still required even without changes.

Question 98
Which class of mutual fund shares has the highest 12b-1 fees?

Correct Answer: C. Class C

Class C shares typically carry ongoing 12b-1 fees of up to 1%, making them costly long term.

Not Correct Answer(s):

A. Class A – Low 12b-1 fees.
B. Class B – Moderate, and they convert.
D. No-load shares – Very low to none.

Question 99
The minimum holding period to qualify for long-term capital gains is:

Correct Answer: A. More than one year

Any asset held **over** 12 months qualifies for long-term capital gains treatment.

Not Correct Answer(s):
B. 6 months – Not enough.
C. 1 year or less – Short-term.
D. No minimum – Incorrect.

Question 100
An investor who wants low-cost, passive exposure to a broad market index should consider:

Correct Answer: B. Index mutual fund
Index funds have low expenses and broad diversification, making them ideal for passive investors.

Not Correct Answer(s):

A. Sector fund – Narrow focus.
C. Hedge fund – High risk, high cost.
D. Actively managed growth fund – Higher expenses and potential volatility.

APPENDICES

APPENDIX A: GLOSSARY OF KEY TERMS

Term	Definition
Asset Allocation	An investment strategy that balances risk by distributing investments across asset classes.
Breakpoint	A dollar amount at which a volume discount is applied to mutual fund purchases.
Custodian	A financial institution responsible for safeguarding fund assets.
Dividend	A portion of a company's earnings distributed to shareholders.
Expense Ratio	The annual fee expressed as a percentage of assets under management in a mutual fund.
FINRA	Financial Industry Regulatory Authority; a self-regulatory organization for broker-dealers.
Investment Adviser	The professional who manages a mutual fund's portfolio and makes investment decisions.
Letter of Intent (LOI)	A commitment by an investor to invest a certain amount in a fund to receive a reduced sales charge.
NAV (Net Asset Value)	The per-share value of a mutual fund, calculated daily as: (Assets - Liabilities) / Shares Outstanding.
Prospectus	A formal document that provides details about a mutual fund or investment offering.
Sales Load	A commission or fee charged when purchasing or redeeming mutual fund shares.
12b-1 Fee	An annual marketing or distribution fee included in a fund's expense ratio.

APPENDIX B: QUICK REFERENCE FORMULAS AND CONCEPTS

1. Net Asset Value (NAV)

NAV= (Total Assets–Liabilities)/Shares Outstanding

2. Public Offering Price (POP)

For Class A shares:

POP=NAV/ (1–Sales Load)

3. Sales Charge Percentage

Sales Charge % =(POP–NAV)/POP

4. Current Yield (for bonds)

Current Yield=Annual Interest Payment/Market Price

5. Price-to-Earnings (P/E) Ratio

P/E Ratio=Market Price per Share/Earnings per Share (EPS

6. Capital Gains Tax Basics

- Short-term: Held for 1 year or less → taxed as ordinary income
- Long-term: Held over 1 year → taxed at preferential rates

APPENDIX C: TEST-TAKING TIPS AND STRATEGIES

1. Understand the Exam Format

- Series 6: 50 questions, 90 minutes
- Series 63: 65 questions, 75 minutes (60 scored)

2. Prioritize High-Yield Topics

Focus more on:

- Mutual fund structures
- Suitability

- State securities laws
- Advertising and communication rules

3. Use Process of Elimination

- Rule out obviously incorrect answers.
- Choose between remaining options using key concepts.

4. Time Management

- Don't spend more than 1–1.5 minutes per question.
- Mark and skip tough questions to revisit later.

5. Read Questions Carefully

- Watch for words like "NOT," "EXCEPT," "MOST LIKELY."
- Focus on what is being asked, not what you assume.

6. Take Practice Exams

- Mimic test conditions (time, silence, no interruptions).
- Review wrong answers and learn from explanations.

7. Day Before the Exam

- Do light review only. Sleep well.
- Organize ID, test confirmation, and arrive early.

APPENDIX D: ADDITIONAL RESOURCES AND READING MATERIALS

Books & Study Guides

- Kaplan Series 6 and 63 Study Guide
- Securities Institute of America Exam Prep Series
- Pass the 63: A Plain English Explanation

Online Platforms

- FINRA: www.finra.org
- NASAA (Series 63): www.nasaa.org

- Investopedia: www.investopedia.com
- Quizlet flashcards for Series 6 & 63
- YouTube channels for securities licensing explanations

Apps and Tools

- Achievable Series 6 & 63 Study App
- STC Interactive Test Bank
- Solomon Exam Prep App

REFERENCES

1. Financial Industry Regulatory Authority (FINRA). www.finra.org
2. North American Securities Administrators Association (NASAA). www.nasaa.org
3. U.S. Securities and Exchange Commission (SEC). www.sec.gov
4. Investment Company Act of 1940.
5. Securities Act of 1933.
6. Securities Exchange Act of 1934.
7. Uniform Securities Act (USA).
8. Kaplan Financial Education. Series 6 and 63 Study Materials.
9. Solomon Exam Prep. Series 6 and Series 63 Study Guide.
10. Pass the 63: A Plain English Explanation, Robert Walker.
11. STCUSA. Securities Training Corporation Series 6 & 63.
12. Achievable Exam Prep Platform. www.achievable.me
13. Investopedia. www.investopedia.com
14. The Balance. www.thebalance.com
15. Series 6 Top-Off Exam Content Outline, FINRA.
16. Series 63 Uniform Securities Agent State Law Exam Outline, NASAA.
17. Wiley. Series 6 Exam Review Guide.
18. McGraw-Hill. Securities Licensing Exam Textbooks.
19. Lorman Education Services. Securities Regulation Webinars.
20. ExamFX. Series 6 & 63 Prep Courses.
21. Bloomberg Financial Glossary.
22. CFA Institute. Investment Foundations.

23. American Association of Individual Investors (AAII). www.aaii.com
24. Securities Industry Essentials (SIE) Exam Prep Guide, Kaplan.
25. Morningstar. Mutual Fund Research and Analysis.
26. U.S. Department of the Treasury. www.treasury.gov
27. NerdWallet. Investment Strategies and Tools.
28. Moneychimp. Financial Calculators and Concepts.
29. FINRA Rule 2210 – Communications with the Public.
30. FINRA Rule 2040 – Payments to Unregistered Persons.
31. FINRA Rule 4512 – Customer Account Information.
32. NASAA Model Rules. Model Rules for Securities Industry.
33. IRS Publication 550 – Investment Income and Expenses.
34. U.S. Government Accountability Office. Financial Regulation Reports.
35. Wall Street Journal. Markets and Mutual Funds Section.
36. Securities Class Action Clearinghouse (SCAC).
37. Federal Reserve Education. www.federalreserveeducation.org
38. CFP Board. Code of Ethics and Standards of Conduct.
39. Bureau of Labor Statistics – Occupational Outlook for Financial Advisors.
40. FINRA Investor Education Foundation. www.finrafoundation.org
41. SEC Investor.gov. Investor Tools and Publications.
42. FINRA BrokerCheck. www.brokercheck.finra.org
43. John C. Bogle, Common Sense on Mutual Funds.
44. Richard Ferri, The Power of Passive Investing.
45. Burton Malkiel, A Random Walk Down Wall Street.
46. Series 6 & 63 Exam Prep – YouTube Channels (TestGeek, Series 7 Whisperer)
47. FINRA Investor Alerts – Understanding Mutual Fund Fees.
48. NASAA Reports on Investment Adviser Activity.
49. The College for Financial Planning. Licensing Program Materials.
50. Investopedia Academy – Series 6 & 63 Crash Course.

www.ingramcontent.com/pod-product-compliance
Lightning Source LLC
LaVergne TN
LVHW090315210926
848480LV00001B/258